The Browser's Guide to EROTICA

The Browser's Guide to EROTICA

ROY HARLEY LEWIS

ST. MARTIN'S PRESS • NEW YORK

For information, write: St. Martin's Press,
175 Fifth Avenue, New York, N.Y. 10010
Manufactured in the United States of America

Library of Congress Cataloging in Publication Data

Lewis, Roy Harley.
Browser's guide to erotica.

1. Erotic literature. I. Title.
HQ462.L48 1982 808.8'03538 81-14576
ISBN 0-312-10672-6 AACR2

Contents

	Preface	6
1	Sniff the Bouquet	9
2	The Author at Bay	23
3	Authors in Erotic Mood	43
4	The Good Old Days . . . And Before	61
5	Fun . . . and Trouble	87
6	Darkest Before the Dawn (1850–1950)	108
7	'Modern' Erotica	122
8	Humour in Erotica	143
9	Not Always Cheap But Usually Nasty . . .	157
10	Artists, Publishers and Collectors	171
11	What Turns You On?	183
12	Looking for Erotic Books	186
	Source Material	192
	Acknowledgements	195
	Index	196

Preface

Time is becoming the great enemy of man's leisure interests as we approach the end of the century. Too much time for those who have no interests; too little for the rest of us. The bibliophile, for example, cannot keep pace with the numbers of books being published each year, let alone catch up with the treasures of the past. Much of the joy of collecting antiquarian books is the thrill of the hunt, but since it can take years to unearth just one rare item, a lifetime of searching doesn't reach back very far.

Erotic books are the most difficult of all to track down; many of them were published in secret, often with a pseudonym disguising the publisher's name and a false address, Amsterdam instead of Paris, for example, or vice versa. Identified titles that have survived (and that merit survival) are then 'lost' in the reserved sections of certain libraries or in the private collections of rich men.

Over 5000 titles are listed in the *Registrum Librorum Eroticorum*, and there may well be almost as many again – occasionally books of literary merit – which have escaped the notice of even the specialist bibliographer. With any specialist subject, the further one investigates the more complex the subject becomes, and erotica are enveloped in greater mystery than most. Scholarly books such as Gershon Legman's *The Horn Book* read like detective stories, the author patiently unravelling layer after layer of rumour and distorted fact to get at the truth. Without Legman's knowledge and dedication – or, let's just say with my lazier disposition – I prefer to browse as the mood takes me, and concentrate on works that interest, excite or amuse me. I have no wish to educate, influence or climb on to a soap-box for any cause. I do hope to entertain.

Having declared that I have no axe to grind, which is true, the only indulgence I have allowed myself is a dislike of people who take the enormously complex topic of pornography too seriously. The so-called liberal is usually just as depressing in this respect as the reactionary he claims to despise. Earnestness, or solemnity, should be discouraged at all costs. Euripides phrased it rather more succinctly in *Alcestis* over 2000 years ago:

> . . . To all solemn and frowning men
> Life is not life, I say, but a disaster.

In the eighteenth century, Voltaire was telling Frederick the Great that solemnity was a disease, yet there still seems little sign of a cure. It affects the expert even more than the ordinary well-meaning idiot. And since sexuality is synonymous with eroticism, one cannot avoid reference to Sigmund Freud. Some people regard Freud as God – I have an American friend who carries his works around the world as others might a Bible – well, maybe a toothbrush. Leaving aside Freud's merits as a psychiatrist, what some of us find objectionable is that he could take the most innocuous, even ridiculous situation – a man slipping on a banana skin – and pompously attach to them the most unlikely motivations, preferably of a sexual connotation. This solemnity is captured in a novel by one Luke Rhinehart (a pseudonym of George Cockroft) called *The Dice Man*. The story is related in the first person by Luke, a psychiatrist in the book, who describes the start of the day thus:

> . . . the world was as near perfect as it ever gets. Freud calls it a state of ego-less polymorphous perversity and frowned upon it, but I have little doubt he never had Lil's hands gliding over him. Or his wife's either for that matter. Freud was a very great man, but I never get the impression that anyone ever effectively stroked his penis . . .

That extract is here merely to emphasise the point about solemnity. But coincidentally, *The Dice Man* is the sort of novel I feel almost an obligation to promote (not that it needs any help), since it has been a constant source of amazement that some do-gooder has never tried to have it suppressed on the grounds of obscenity, gambling or even medical malpractice. It was one of the 70s' most riveting novels.

My view that there is no such thing as pornography – whatever dictionary definition you care to apply – only good writing and bad is borne out by no less an authority than Maurice Girodias, founder of Olympia Press. In an essay, 'More Heat Than Light', contained in an anthology *To Deprave and Corrupt . . .*, Girodias – who must be given credit for introducing many now famous writers, including such establishment figures as Samuel Beckett and Vladimir Nabokov – wrote on the difference between a 'pornographic' novel and a 'non-pornographic' one:

> Technically the problems are identical – style, plot, construction, dialogue etc. The themes are the same: I suppose that the human passions constitute the theme of at least 95 per cent of the novels which are being published today.
>
> Naturally, quality varies. But in each category there exists parallel scales of value, e.g. you can have a *bad* non-pornographic novel and *good* pornographic one – the final qualification depending exclusively on the talent and intelligence of the author. . . .
>
> The final difference between the two categories lies only in the scope of language used, rather than anything else: the adoption of taboo words by the one kind of writer, and their exclusion by the other; and even more deeply, in the vivid description of sexual impulses and actions by the one category, and the painstaking circumnavigation of such subjects by the other . . .

Whether we agree with Girodias or not, what do we mean by 'good' and 'bad' writing? While it should be possible to judge the written word by academic standards, literature has little to do with grammar or precedent. What would school examiners have made of the emerging James Joyce? Besides, different people are affected in different ways. Unlike a television receiver which presents the same picture to every viewer (*almost* the same), words on a page are assembled by the eyes and mind of each reader in slightly different patterns, and in different time-scales.

Perhaps the truth lies in the difference between writing that has integrity and the artificial or sham, but the debate will continue with little hope of a universally acceptable conclusion, because decisions of this sort will always be very personal. Browsing, by definition, is inevitably superficial by standards of scholarship, but I've managed to cover a fair bit of ground in selecting the works that give me satisfaction and amusement. I invite you to share that experience.

1
Sniff the Bouquet

Whether the underlying attraction of quality erotica is its scarcity, like vintage wines – whether, that is, a regular diet would dull the palate – is debatable. Frequent exposure to anything has an overkill effect. The proliferation of political slogans scrawled on walls – 'Stop the killing/oppression in . . .' (perm any two from fifty-two) or 'This degrades women' – simply means that the message eventually fails to register. In the sexual context it tends to lower the levels of what is morally acceptable, and more significantly loses the power to arouse. Although I cannot vouch for the authenticity of the following story about Anglo-Saxon Britain, it serves to prove my point.

It seems that three Viking sailing ships raiding the east coast of England beached in quick succession, the first and second in immaculate formation, the men jumping out smartly, eager for the fray, swords, axes and armour highly polished, morale 101 per cent – walking advertisements for the life of the ninth-century adventurer. The third ship, however, disgorged a very motley crew, unkempt, undisciplined and obviously exhausted. They staggered on to the English sand, intent on one thing only – sleep. But waving his sword theatrically, the commanding officer issued fresh orders: 'Men from the first ship are on pillaging duty; men from the second ship on looting. . . .'

'Oh no,' groaned the captain of the third ship, 'not raping for us again!'

The same might be said of the soft-porn magazine market where, in an effort to go one step further than the competition, to be even more bizarre, some publishers in the 1970s resorted to illustrations that most of their readers probably found distasteful. Most of the porn that is readily available these days is of the cheap and nasty sort. Like many things produced for the volume market to satisfy a guaranteed demand, it clinically gathers together the basic ingredients, yet manages to assemble a finished product that is functional but unrefined, a shoddy imitation, not an original. With most consumer products a production-line article can represent good value for money, but in literature, as in all the arts, it is originality and artistry that set standards. Nor can there ever be any substitute for quality.

Cheap does not necessarily mean nasty, but in western society, especially the United Kingdom, the influences of traditional class snobbery extend to issues of law. It is widely believed that in many courts, particularly those presided over by Justices of the Peace – seldom professional judges – the so-called middle-class white-collar executive can have an advantage over the so-called lower-class blue-collar worker, being credited with a greater awareness of social responsibility. In the same way, the attitude of 'Authority' to the sale of shoddily-produced soft porn will often differ from its assessment of similar material sumptuously produced in a limited edition and selling at (say) £100 a volume, the inference being that anyone who can afford that sort of money is less likely to be corrupted or depraved.

Attitudes to erotica have another relationship to class structure, but in the opposite sense, since there seems to be less interest among blue-collar workers than among the middle classes. It has been said by a number of authorities that the dirty limerick, for example, for many years a dying folk art, has been kept alive by the college graduate, particularly in the United States.

Attitudes are, of course, linked to behaviour patterns in society. *Time* is a major consideration: what was obscene yesterday is acceptable today, yet may be obscene again tomorrow. History is littered with such cycles, which I'll try to illustrate in due course. The hoary political arguments about 'freedom' need not be discussed here, except to comment on how much the ideologies of Left and Right have in common when it comes to protecting the interests of their subjects. In 1978, the South African Publications Appeal Board, in a rush of blood to the head, lifted a fourteen-year ban on Harold Robbins' *The Carpetbaggers*, presumably having decided it was no longer 'offensive and harmful to public morals'.

We should also try to distinguish between the 'public' and individual points of view. What is emotionally or sexually exciting to one person is as mundane as chewing gum to someone else. There are references in Harold Robbins' books to a wide variety of common sexual diversions, not to say perversions – perhaps on the grounds that you can't please everyone but you can have a damned good try. To do his job properly, the censor should know that it is not only these popular sexual fetishes that, when recaptured in print, have a damaging effect on the public; he should also realise that an ostensibly innocuous passage such as 'I introduced myself and shook his hand warmly' could easily stir the suppressed passions of hundreds of men and women with subconscious hang-ups about the hand, which (some might say) has powerful sexual associations. I cannot reveal the title of the novel including this sentence in case some local authority should suddenly wake up to its responsibilities and decide to ban the book.

The first organised group in the United Kingdom (only just beating the USA) to take it upon themselves to *save* mankind – in other words, to stop people from enjoying themselves – was an august seventeenth-century body called The Societies for the Reformation of Manners. Their duties were many – from the prevention of Sabbath-breaking to sodomy (prevention of) – and their energies set standards for similar societies in the past 300 years, although these influences have gradually waned. Few of us these days have time for prudes and busybodies who try to impose narrow views on the rest of society, yet there is a surprising streak of puritanism, in one form or another, in most men and women who regard themselves as 'enlightened' or liberal in their attitudes towards sex and literature. Frankness comes in layers, and for most of us the layers are thinner than we care to admit. Why else, when reviewing our most intimate thoughts, do so many of us feel the need for additional privacy, for caution and even a form of mental censorship?

If exiled to a desert island with a limited number of books, I should insist on including the Diaries of Samuel Pepys, for whom my affection over the years has remained constant. The little man is admirable for his integrity in business (among many attributes) and for his frankness in admitting shortcomings. Yet was he not also a hypocrite? Pepys wrote from the heart, without the judicious editing of other diarists concerned with publication. Never imagining the diaries would be read by anyone, he was invariably honest with himself, yet was incongruously reticent in certain passages – on matters for which he felt varying degrees of sensitivity. He was not ashamed to admit chasing women, for example, 'playing' with their breasts or having 'his way'. Yet the following is typical of him in another mood:

> I by water to Westminster Hall and there did see Mrs Lane, and de là, elle and I to the cabaret at the Cloche in the street du roy; and there; after some caresses, je l'ay foutée sous de la chaise deux times, and the last to my great pleasure; mais j'ai grand peur que je l'ai fait faire aussi elle même. Mais after I had done, elle commençait parler as before and I did perceive that je n'avais fait rien de danger à elle. Et avec ça, I came away; and though I did make grand promises à la contraire, nonobstant je ne la verrai pas long time.
>
> So home to supper and to bed – with my mind un peu troublé pour ce que j'ai fait today. But I hope it will be la dernière de toute ma vie.
>
> (16 January 1664)

Since the diary was written in shorthand and is therefore difficult to decipher in any case, there was no practical need to switch to a hotchpotch of French and English. Yet adultery was obviously a sensitive issue to Pepys; he was seeing it as a betrayal of his wife (in this case for the first time, and therefore a traumatic experience), not to mention the real fear of an unwanted pregnancy.

The way that Pepys's mind was 'conditioned' by concern for his wife is revealed in the diary after the terrible showdown nearly five years later when Elizabeth Pepys discovered his more serious relationship with their servant Deb. Nothing less than his complete humiliation would satisfy her and when a couple of nights later she graciously bestowed her favours, he wrote (19 November 1668): 'and so to supper, and pretty kind words, and to bed, and there *yo did hazer con ella* to her content. . . .' Thoughts of making love to his wife did not normally inhibit Pepys, but the highly charged atmosphere adds to his insecurity – and the delicate relationship with Elizabeth (more than the sex act) was a subject he could no longer talk about in a relaxed manner. Most of us can only act and speak frankly when we do not feel vulnerable to outside influences.

In his fascinating *Case Books of Simon Forman: Sex and Society in Shakespeare's Age*, A. L. Rowse adds further colour, especially on moral attitudes, to the picture he has already painted of Elizabethan times, long before we were plagued with censorship. Forman, a doctor and astrologer, was a more aggressive (and more successful) seducer than Pepys, yet like him referred to most of his sexual conquests with extreme discretion – in more detail perhaps, but in Latin! In both cases we're dealing not with public statements, but with confessions made in privacy – people talking in confidence to themselves and, more relevantly, to their own consciences.

Of course it might be argued that these double standards simply show hypocrisy in another guise. John Wilmot, second Earl of Rochester (1647–80), whose life makes fascinating reading, was one of Charles II's most disreputable friends, yet he has been described as one of the finest lyrical and satirical poets of the age. Much of his writing verges on the obscene (whether it goes over the edge depends on your point of view), and there is no question that Rochester enjoyed his notoriety. But somewhat out of character, shortly before he died at the age of thirty-three (hardly surprisingly from VD), he ordered that everything questionable be burnt. Rochester was probably more concerned with his reputation at the eleventh hour than with making his peace with God, despite what his confessors claimed – yet why? Most of this material was in circulation (at least in manuscript form), so it was copied and much of it has survived.

A typical example of Rochester's contempt for romanticism, and particularly the love songs that had gone out of fashion, was the satirical 'The Wish':

Oh, that I now cou'd by some Chymic Art
To Sperm convert my Vitals and my Heart,
That at one Thrust I might my Soul translate,
And in the Womb myself regenerate;
There steep'd in Lust, nine Months I would remain
Then boldly fuck my passage out again.

His five-act play *Sodom: or The Quintessence of Debauchery*, although not published until four years after his death, had had at least one performance before Charles II and his court and presumably raised few eyebrows, even though many of the characters were reputedly based on his friends there. The cast list alone was explicit enough:

DRAMATIS PERSONAE

Bolloxinion – King of Sodom
Cuntigratia – Queen
Picket – Prince
Swivia – Princess
Buggeranthos – General of the Army
Pockenello – Prince, Colonel & Favourite of the King
Borastus Buggermaster General
Pine
Twely Two Pimps of Honour
Fuckadilla
Officina
Cunticula Maids of Honour
Clitoris
Flux – Physician to the King
Virtuoso – Merkin and Dildoe Maker to the Royal Family
Boys, Rogues, Pimps and Other Attendants

The following extract is inoffensive enough, but it vividly captures the philosophy of Bolloxinion, King of Sodom, and a comparison with Rochester's crony Charles II is inevitable:

Thus in the zenith of my lust I reign;
I eat to swive, and swive to eat again;
Let other monarchs, who their sceptres bear
To keep their subjects less in love than fear
Be salves to crowns, my nation shall be free;
My pintle only shall my sceptre be,
My laws shall act more pleasure than command,
And with my prick I'll govern the land.

A few years after his death, British laws suffered a change of heart and publishers of his works were prosecuted, although that eventuality was probably furthest from Rochester's mind when he asked for their destruction.

Why people are embarrassed by reality is a big subject, but an examination of the meaning of the word 'prude' is interesting. The dictionary definition refers (controversially) to 'a woman of squeamish propriety in regard to the relations of the sexes', and this unfortunate image was anticipated by Thomas Morton (*c.*1764–1838) who created Mrs Grundy, the arbiter of English

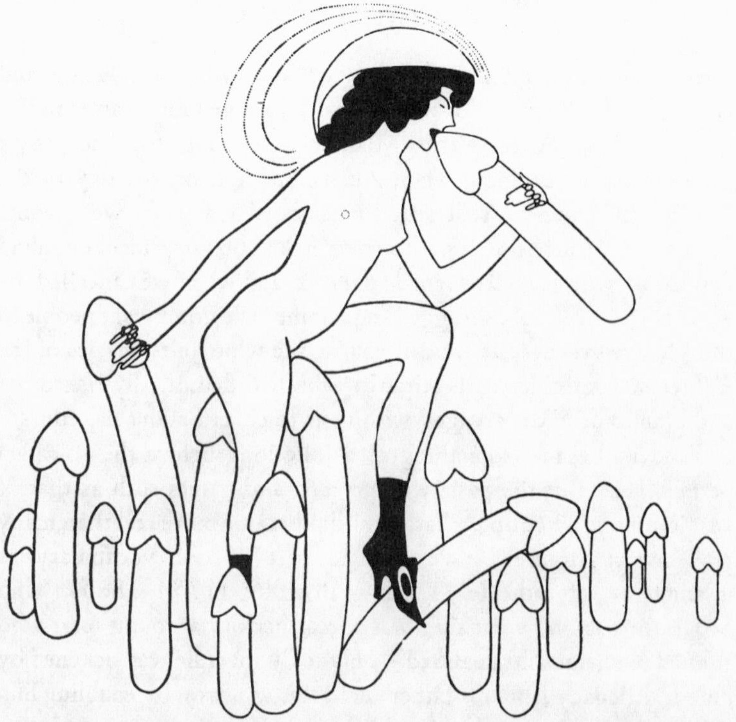

The distinctive style of German artist Max Klinger (1857–1920), who seems to have had a mild obsession with the sex organs, is shown in this illustration from a limited edition of the Earl of Rochester's *Sodom*

respectability, in his play *Speed the Plough* (1798), and substantiated by the American, Ambrose Bierce (1842–*c.*1914), who wrote 'A prude is one who blushes modestly at the indelicacy of *her* thoughts, and virtuously flees from the temptation of *her* desires' (my italics).

If we accept that one cannot differentiate between prudes of either sex, we cannot even restrict the use of the word to 'the relations of the sexes'. Words having no such relationship can be just as offensive to those who look for offence. In 1962, the postal authorities in the United Kingdom refused the Collins Crime Club permission to advertise on the outside of envelopes a book called *Bloody Instructions* because that first word – defined by the dictionary as being smeared with a red liquid circulating in the veins of higher animals – might 'offend quite a number of people'.

Even in matters unrelated to sex or language, there are over-sensitive people who seek to protect their 'dignity' by drawing a veil across innocent activities. Some years ago, when producing and writing Pathé Pictorial for the cinema, I arranged for a camera crew to film West African tribal dancers preparing for the Royal Tournament in London. To my consternation, on the day of the filming, the dancers' representative insisted that they wear white singlets. His concern was not to cover naked breasts, since the ruling applied to male as well as female dancers, and when we cancelled the film session, he simply shrugged, explaining 'We don't want people to think we're savages'. It was, of course, the white missionaries of the eighteenth and nineteenth centuries who had dedicatedly risked life and limb to provide 'savages' with vests to cover Satan's nakedness.

Prudery became something of a joke long before the so-called permissiveness of the past twenty years, and names such as that of Mrs Grundy, a fictitious character who became more real than many real historic figures, have become part of our vocabulary as instruments of ridicule. Thomas Bowdler (1754–1825), who bequeathed us 'bowdlerism', was a real person, a young man who studied medicine and qualified – only to discover he was sickened by illness! A legacy from his father cured this affliction by enabling him to give it up and apply his equally dubious talents to curing the excesses of literature. His first major contribution to public morality appeared in 1807 with his ten-volume *Family Shakespeare*, in which 'those words and expressions are omitted which cannot with propriety be read aloud in a family'. In fact, although it was this blue-pencil job that made his name, he was not the first to expurgate Shakespeare, that 'honour' going to Alexander Pope almost a century before. (Ironically, many of the works of Pope were in turn censored by nineteenth-century editors.) But not content with fiction, which in some eyes may not be sacrosanct, Dr Bowdler then censored Gibbon's *History of the Decline and Fall of the Roman Empire*, 'with the careful omissions of all passages of an irreligious or immoral tendency'.

It was at the start of the nineteenth-century that the climate of public opinion enabled bowdlerism to flourish. In their first edition of the *Family Shakespeare*, Dr Bowdler and his sister Harriet (considered to have done most of the work) applied their blue pencils to practically every play, but decided that *Romeo and Juliet* was beyond redemption and left it out altogether, although an edited version appeared in the second edition of 1818. By the end of the century there were nearly fifty expurgated editions of Shakespeare.

Other popular writers suffered the same fate, and in *Dr Bowdler's Legacy* Noel Perrin illustrates the extent to which ordinary people took expurgation seriously with an anecdote about Henry Fielding's *Tom Jones*. He reveals that in 1886 one critic described the book as so indecent that 'a Bowdlerised version would scarcely be intelligible'. Whereupon, ten years later, by coincidence or not, Fielding's own great-granddaughter took up the challenge and produced one.

Jonathan Swift was another target for the censors who took on Bowdler's mantle. Swift had been infuriated by the way his printer Benjamin Motte had 'basely mangled and abused' the text of *Gulliver's Travels* (1726), although his own changes to Motte's version were not discovered until 1976 (see my *Antiquarian Books: An Insider's Account*). But Motte had been terrified of legal repercussions from Swift's *political* satire. The nineteenth-century tampering with *Gulliver's Travels* (there were 150 editions in that period) was motivated by his use of 'wicked' language. Objection was taken to references, for example, to the hairy yahoos being bald on their buttocks, except around the anus, to women with breasts that sagged so much they reached almost to the ground. Another shocking and 'unnecessary' passage was the description of the Lilliputian army marching under Gulliver's legs and looking up at his genitals. Looking was surely the height of bad taste – but their reaction (half were amused and the other half agog with admiration!) took it beyond the pale.

But, as I suggested earlier, it is not only bad language or irreligious and immoral behaviour that offends some people. An enthusiastic expurgator in the early nineteenth century was the Rev. James Plumptre, to whom the subject matter, or *tone*, of a story was of prime importance. Plumptre turned his attention from the Bible to plays, books and poetry; the end to which he worked was the propagation of good and moral behaviour, and not only in sexual matters. A hero who was not modest at all times or was even too aggressive in the battle against villainy, and lower-class folk who were not respectful to their betters, presented challenges for his improvements. (Presumably, for example, he would have overcome the problem of Mellors, the gamekeeper–lover of Lady Chatterley, by making him an aristocrat, perhaps a foreign Royal down on his luck.) Plumptre even had a go at Defoe's *Robinson Crusoe*, which seems unbelievable, although the attention given to his *Moll Flanders* (1722) is slightly more understandable by Victorian standards – if only for its title: *Moll, or The Fortunes and Misfortunes of the Famous Moll Flanders, who was born in Newgate, and during a Life of continued Variety, for Threescore Years, besides her Childhood, was Twelve Year a Whore, five times a Wife (whereof once to her own Brother), Twelve Year a Thief, Eight Year a transported felon in Virginia, at last grew Rich, liv'd Honest, and died a Penitent.* Moll and *Roxana* (1724) were both prostitutes, but there is not a truly erotic line in either book. As Noel Perrin in *Dr Bowdler's Legacy* points out, when the latter was published in the United States in 1924 it was introduced by the distinguished critic and novelist Willa Cather as 'safe as sterilized gauze'.

But even the most innocent of books have not escaped expurgation over the years. In England these include *Moby Dick* (not because of the title, but because of incidental references to other dirty words, such as underclothes); in the United States, *Tom Brown's Schooldays* (not because of the scenes of sadism, which were typical of an English public school of the time, or for overtones of homosexuality, but because of a reference to the boys drinking beer), and *The Adventures of Huckleberry Finn*, because of the hero's slang expressions and colloquialisms. The last is especially interesting because Mark Twain (Samuel Clemens), a masterly storyteller of children's yarns (children, that is, from eight to eighty), was not above a little vulgarity on occasion. Twain was a fan of Samuel Pepys and between publishing *Tom Sawyer* (1876) and *Huckleberry Finn* (1884), he wrote a delightful dairy piece on the court of Elizabeth I, with the famous names of the period in attendance. Called *1601*, it was written principally for the pleasure of a close friend (a clergyman!) and was then rejected with consternation by the editor to whom it was submitted. In 1880 it was privately printed in pamphlet form by another friend, John Hay, who later became Secretary of State. The first hardback version was published at another bastion of respectability, West Point, the United States Military Academy!

Despite the freshness of Tom and Huck, and his *A Connecticut Yankee in King Arthur's Court* (1889), history does not do credit to the wit of Clemens. His *1601*, or to use the full title *A Conversation as*

It Was by the Social Fireside in the Time of the Tudors, might be described as scatology, as distinct from erotica, but it is delightful enough to justify the inclusion of the following extracts:

> In ye heate of ye talke, it befel that one did breake wynde, yielding an exceeding mightie and distressful stinke, wherat all did laffe full sore, and then:
>
> **Ye Queene**: Verily, in mine eight and sixty yeares have I not hearde ye fellow to this fartte. Meseemeth by ye greate sound and clamour of it, it was male yet ye bellie it did lurke behinde should now falle lene and flat against ye spine of him that hath been delivered of so stately and so vaste a bulke, whereas ye guts of them that doe quiff-splitters beare, stand comely, stille and rounde. Prithee, let ye author confess ye offspring. Will my Lady Alice testify?
>
> . . . (Then there was silence, and each did turne him toward ye worshipful Sir Walter Ralegh, that browned, embattled, bloody swashbuckler, who rousing up did smile and simpering say):
>
> **Ralegh**: Most gracious Majestie, 'twas I that did it; but, indeed, it was so poor and fragile a note compared with such as I am wont to furnish, that in sooth I was ashamed to call ye weakling mine in so august a Presence. It was nothing – less than nothing – Madame. I did it but to clear my nether throat; but hadde I come prepared then hadde I delivered something worthie. Beare with me, please your Grace, till I can make amends.
>
> Then delivered he himself of such a godlesse and rock-shivering blaste, that all were fain to stop their ears, and following it did come so dense and foul a stinke, that that which went before did seem a poor and trifling thing beside it . . . Then saith he, feigning that he blushed and was confused, 'I perceive that I am weake today and cannot justice doe unto my powers,' and sat him down as who should say, – 'There, it is not much; yet he that hath an arse to spare, let him follow that, an' he think he can.'
>
> . . . Then fell they to talk about the manners and customs of many peoples, and master Shaxpur spake of ye booke by Sir Michael Montaine, wherein was mention of ye custom of ye widows of Perigord, to wear upon ye head-dress, in sign of widowhood, a jewel in ye similitude of a man's member wilted and limber, whereat ye Queene did laffe and say, widows in England do wear

prickers too, but 'twixt ye thyghs and not wilted either, till coition hath done that office for them. Master Shaxpur did also observe that the Sieur de Montaine hath also spoken of a certain emperor of such mightie prowess that he did take ten maiden-heddes in ye compass of a single night, the while his empress did entertain two and twenty lusty knights atween her sheets and yet was not satisfied; whereat ye merrie Countess Granby saith, a ram is yet ye Emperor's superior, since he will top above a hundred ewes 'twixt sun and sun, and after, if he can have none more to shag, will masturbate until he hath enryched whole acres with hys seed.

Then spake ye damned wynd-mill, Sir Walter, of a people in ye uttermost parts of America, that copulate not until they be five and thirty yeares of age, ye women being eight and twenty, and do it then but once in seven yeares.

. . . (Then spake ye Queene of how she met old Rabelais when she was turned fifteen, and hee did tell her of a man his father knew that hadde a double pair of bollocks, whereon a controversy followed as concerning ye moste just way to spell ye word, ye controversy running high 'twixt ye learned Bacon and ye ingenious Jonson, until at last ye olde Lady Margery, wearying of it all, saith, 'Gentles, what mattereth it how ye spell ye word? I warrant ye when ye use your bollocks ye shall not think of it; and my Lady Granby, bee ye content, let ye spelling be; ye shall enjoy ye beating of them on your buttocks just ye same I trow. Before I had gained my fourteenth yeare, I hadde learned that them that would explore a cunt, stopp'd not to consider ye spelling o't.')

Sir Walter: In sooth, when a shift's turned uppe, delay is meet for naught but dalliance. Boccaccio hath a story of a priest that did beguile a mayd into his cell, then knelt him in a corner for to pray for grace that he been rightly thankful for this tender maiden-hedde the Lord hadde sent him, but the abbot spying through ye keyhole did see a tuft of brownish hair with fair white flesh about it, wherefore, when ye priest's prayer was done his chance was gone, forasmuch as ye little mayd hadde but ye one cunt and that was already occupied to her content.

As attitudes change (albeit in cycles) certain words become acceptable, and these days surely no one turns a hair at 'legs', whereas decent people (*their* designation, not mine) would once find it embarrassing to specify which of the four 'limbs' they were talking about. We certainly don't refer to a 'male cow' or 'lady dog' when we mean bull and bitch, and we can say in any company, without the hint of a blush, 'breasts' and (deep breath) 'knickers'.

'Fuck' is even today more debatable. Included in dictionaries of modern slang and even some ordinary dictionaries (a valid guide to acceptability), the several origins claimed for it include one novel theory posed by James Barke in his *Pornography and Bawdry in Literature and Society*, as 'an onomatopoeic word equivalent to the sound made by the penis in the vagina'. The word is believed to have been used for the first time in literature by the Scottish poet William Dunbar (*c.*1465–*c.*1580) in *A Bout of Wooing* (*c*1503) and several times in Scotland in the sixteenth century. But as Dunbar's original title, *Ane Brash of Wowing*, indicates, the language is as foreign as Chaucer's Middle English, and therefore escaped the scrutiny and subsequent disfavour of the expurgators.

But if 'fuck' is beyond the pale, there are over 1200 English synonyms for the word (all right, so there are 1201!), although some are pretty obscure – such as 'tick-tack', coined in the mid-sixteenth century, and 'jumble', late sixteenth to eighteenth century (which presumably goes to show what *may* have been going on at apparently respectable churches up and down the country for the past 250 years). Naturally, every sexual word has a variety of synonyms, some ingenious and quite charming, others more embarrassing than the original. However the problem is not a literary one; more one of society's attitudes to sexual matters.

During World War II, the British and American governments implemented programmes for combating VD, but had unexpected problems when some newspapers refused to accept even expurgated advertisements. In the United States Catholic pressure groups condemned the campaign for 'making promiscuity safe'. Promiscuity was also encouraged, it was thought, by clothing (or lack of it) and especially the way it was arranged. It is the Victorians who spring to mind for going to extremes with their habit of decorating statues with figleaves, cleaning up artistic impressions for the family – for example by dressing Cupid in a skirt – and even putting covers on inanimate objects such as table-legs, but they were not alone in their prudery.

Fashion through the ages serves as a barometer to moral attitudes. Exposed breasts and even nipples have come, gone and returned, yet it was not until the latter half of the twentieth century that the introduction of the mini-skirt displayed a woman's thighs for the first time in 'dressed' society. It is doubtful that we will ever see a return to the modesty of covered neck, arm (in Pepys's day, ladies at court might not worry about the deepest of plunge necklines, or even a protruding nipple, but would always cover the upper arm) and ankle, let alone the earlier obsession with the bosom (the Church having even referred to the laced openings to the bodice as 'the gates of hell').

Significantly among men, there has never been a return to the fifteenth and sixteenth century fashion of the codpiece, latterly padded to suggestive proportions. Yet who is to say it won't catch on again in the next century? We don't know, but the greatest influence on fashion today is the media, particularly movies, and many styles of the past have enjoyed a revival in this way. At least there is no one around, in the western world, at least, to *tell* us what or what not to wear.

However, let me return to attitudes and the surprising contradictions of modern society. A succinct way of encapsulating the whole subject is the old Scottish joke about Mac and Andy, labourers on a Glasgow building site:

Mac: Whit kind of weeken' did ye have, Andy?
Andy: Fuck'n great, fuck'n fantastic. A went tae the Bawaland ballroom on Saturday nicht an' there wis this fuck'n blonde ther – whit a fuck'n blonde! We get on the fuck'n flair and fuck'n jig, all fuck'n close up. Then inta the fuck'n bar an a few fuck'n rum an peps an mair fuck'n dancin' an mair fuck'n rum an peps and then inta a fuck'n taxi an back tae ma fuck'n place.
Mac: Whit happen'd then, Andy?
Andy: Whit de yae think fuck'n happened? We had sexual intercourse!

2
The Author at Bay

The impact of erotica is cushioned more by the times in which we live than the quality of the writing. Now that we are used to the soft-porn magazine, dominated by less than beautiful open-crotch views, it seems strange that our grandfathers could have been excited by the glimpse of an ankle. Environmental conditioning so influences our reactions to erotic literature that what was once whispered about as 'hot stuff ' seems too tame to be noticed today.

So, what *is* offensive? A graphic description, poetically written, of the conventional kiss can be arousing for some but distasteful if you belong to a tribe which prefers to rub noses. Swear-words are perhaps the best example. Laughable though it now seems, the expletive 'not bloody likely' in George Bernard Shaw's *Pygmalion* represented a peak of daring for several generations, bringing titters from audiences for thirty years or so.

Most of us are inclined to laziness when it comes to a stand on moral issues. We tend to allow others to speak up and then follow that lead. Whose lead do we follow, whose opinions and authority do we accept? Anatole France (1844–1924), a respected literary figure, set one course: 'Of all sexual aberrations, chastity is the strangest.' Shaw may not have argued with that sentiment and certainly he did not bargain for the outcry that greeted *Mrs Warren's Profession* (1898), a study of prostitution, which was suppressed in the United Kingdom by the Lord Chamberlain (it being first produced privately by the Stage Society in 1902, but not publicly until 1925). It is interesting to note that prostitution as a subject has more often than not been grudgingly accepted, but only when the treatment emphasises the sin and degradation and terrible end for the women involved.

An attempt to close the play's production on Broadway, 'stage-managed' by the New York Society for the Suppression of Vice, misfired when the producer shrewdly invited the Society's moving spirit, Anthony Comstock, to the opening night and thus ensured a sell-out. The courts decided that the play was acceptable and it continued to run to capacity audiences. In fact Comstock, who was also a special agent appointed by the Post Office to enforce a Federal Act excluding 'obscene' matter from the mail and making the 'advertising' of such matter an offence, heard of the play only when he was attacked by Shaw, in a row over *Man and Superman*, which the New York Public Library had relegated to the 'reserved' shelves. Shaw assumed that Comstock was to blame and reacted with a letter to the London correspondent of the *New York Times*; the issue of 26 September 1905 ran a front-page headline across two columns: 'Comstockery is the world's outstanding joke at the expense of the United States.' Never one for half measures, Shaw rather contradicted himself by describing the United States as 'only a second-rate, country town civilisation'. But the word thus coined, 'Comstockery', had the desired effect and became part of the language, although Comstock retained much of his authority until his death in 1917, having successfully stopped not only literary works but also useful medical and scientific studies, such as books on birth control.

Whatever the subject, its effect depends less on what is actually written, drawn or photographed than on what happens to that input when 'processed' in our heads: I'm speculating about what it must be like to be blind. Pino Orioli tells the story in *Adventures of a Bookseller* of his first venture in the trade in London's Charing Cross Road before World War I, when one of his most valued customers collected erotica. Apart from a healthy appetite for prints – ranging from those having some aesthetic appeal to crude pornography – he would pay handsomely for 'classics' such as the Works of Pietro Aretino with (Orioli recalls) illustrations by Agostino Caracci, which are much rarer and more explicit than those of Giulio Romano; the *City [sic] of the Plain*, published anonymously in Paris (Orioli's memory was possibly at fault, since the book is described in *Registrum Librorum Eroticorum* as *Sins, The, of the Cities of the Plain, or the Recollections of a Mary-Ann, with short essays on Sodomy and Tribadism*, London, 1881); an illustrated volume of *Les Oeuvres de*

Paphos, and Aubrey Beardsley's *Lysistrata*.

Nothing strange about that, you might think – except that his customer was blind. Orioli was fascinated by the man, a caricature of the blind street beggar, shabbily dressed and bedraggled, unkempt long hair protruding beneath a dirty felt hat, and highly skilled in his 'profession'. The technique was to stand on a corner rattling a couple of pennies in a tin mug, imploring passers-by to 'take pity' on the blind, until he had enough to transfer to his pocket and then start over again. Asked how without eyes he could appreciate the erotica, he said his 'missus' described the drawings and read the prose so graphically that he did not need to see for himself!

So, again, what has been meant by 'hot stuff'? There can be no one acceptable answer that traverses the many different attitudes, but it's interesting and revealing to compare four of the most notorious books published this century, in terms of their contemporary backgrounds. The books, in order of publication, are *The Well of Loneliness* (Radclyffe Hall), *Lady Chatterley's Lover* (D. H. Lawrence), *Tropic of Capricorn* (Henry Miller) and *The Philanderer* (Stanley Kauffmann).

However, before taking a closer look, it will help to examine them in the broad context of censorship. Many books have been written on the subject, but all we need for our purposes is a cursory glance at the significant stages in the history of censorship up to the present day. In the United Kingdom the Crown's first attempt to ban a sexually obscene book (as distinct from those with religious or political content) was in 1708, when *The Fifteen Plagues of a Maidenhead* (nothing to do with VD, but a repetitive description of the number of ways in which a maidenhead might be vulnerable) was brought before the magistrate. The printer was found not guilty, and it was not until 1725 that Edmund Curll (1675–1747) was tried and convicted (although the sentence of a fine and spell in the pillory was not carried out for another two years) for publishing *Venus in the Cloister, or the Nun in Her Smock*. Written many years before, the story related sexual orgies that were permitted by the 'hypocritical' Catholics; in other words, the work of a Protestant indulging in a favourite pastime of the age – Catholic baiting. But the author's style was restrained enough to be mildly erotic in places, as in the following passage where he describes the sexually frustrated nun fighting a losing battle with self-control:

> As soon as Vespers were over, Dosithea, as though she had not been all this while addressing herself to Heaven, went immediately and prostrated herself in her oratory. She prayed, wept, and sighed but all to no purpose. She found herself more oppressed than ever, and in order to insult anew and with greater violence that opinionated nature, takes her discipline in hand, and pulling up her coats and smock to her very navel, and tying them about her with a girdle, she had no mercy upon her poor thighs and that which had caused all her sufferings, which then lay entirely bare and uncovered. This rage having lasted some time, her strength failed her by this cruel act, she had scarce so much left as to set her clothes at liberty, which exposed her more than half naked. She rested her head upon her mattress, and making reflection upon the stage of poor mortals, which she called miserable and wretched, being born with such movements which they condemned, though it was impossible to repress them, she fell into a very great weariness, but it was an amorous one which the fury of her passion had caused and made this young thing taste such a pleasure which ravished her to the very skies. At this moment, nature, inciting all its forces, broke through all the obstacles which opposed its sallies, and that virginity which till then had been in prison, delivered it without any aid of succour, with the utmost impetuosity, leaving its keeper extended on the floor as a certain sign of her being discomfited. . . . Thou woudst have seen that innocent half naked, her mouth smiling with those amorous, gentle contractions of which she knew not the cause. Thou woudst have seen her in an ecstasy, her eyes half dying, and without any strength or vigour fall beneath the laws of undisguised nature, and lose in defiance to all her care that treasure, the keeping of which had cost her so much pain and trouble.

Coincidentally, Curll seems to have entered publishing respectably enough in the year that *Fifteen Plagues* was prosecuted, with *An Explication of a Famous Passage in the Dialogue of St Justin Martyr with Typhon, concerning the Immortality of Human Souls*, which began a specialisation in religious books. However, Curll was a hustler and would not hesitate to pirate anything he thought might have a market. Henry Curwen in a *History of Booksellers* (1873) describes one such incident:

> . . . A Latin discourse had been pronounced at the funeral of

Robert South by the captain of Westminster School, and Curll, thinking it would be readily purchased by the public, reprinted it – without permission, and, more important, failing to check the Latin thereby aroused the anger of the Westminster scholars, who enticed him into Dean's Yard on the pretence of giving him a more perfect copy; there, he met with a college salutation, for he was first presented with the ceremony of the blanket, in which when the skeleton had been well shook, he was carried in triumph to the school, and, after receiving a mathematical construction for his false concords, he was re-conducted to Dean's Yard, and on his knees asking pardon of the aforesaid Mr Barber (the captain whose Latin he had murdered) for his offence, he was kicked out the yard, and left to the huzzas of the rabble.

In the same year (1716) it appears that he was summoned before the House of Lords for publishing *An Account of the Trial of the Earl of Winton*, a breach of the standing orders.

He could be shrewd. After publishing the *Poems* of the Earl of Rochester, in unexpurgated form, he sent a copy to a Dr Robinson, Bishop of London, an incident reported by Henry Curwen thus: 'and a request that his Lordship would please revise the interleaved volume as he thought fit; but the bishop, not to be caught, smiled and said, "I am told that Mr Curll is a shrewd man, and should I revise the book you have brought, he would publish it as approved by me".'

John Nichols (1745–1826) in his *Literary Anecdotes* writes:

> The memory of Edmund Curll has been transmitted to posterity with an obloquy more severe than he deserved. Whatever were his demerits in having occasionally published works that the present age would very properly consider too licentious, he certainly deserves commendation for his industry in preserving our national remains. And it may, perhaps, be added, that he did not publish a single volume but what, amidst a profusion of base metal, contained some precious ore, some valuable reliques, which future collectors could nowhere else have found.

History has dismissed Curll as a pornographer and he is remembered principally for his denunciation, along with others, in *The Dunciad* by Alexander Pope, a genius by common assent, but an unpleasant character.

The *last* all-embracing censor in the United Kingdom was the

Lord Chamberlain, appointed by the monarch to carry out a number of useless functions, the most dangerous of which was to protect theatre audiences from the blasphemies and obscenities of playwrights and producers. (Film censorship still exists, but on a voluntary basis and is far less iniquitous.) The Lord Chamberlain's powers were abolished in 1968, giving the theatre freedom to use its own good sense for the first time in 231 years. When the appointment was first made, the principal concern was to safeguard the dignity of the monarch, and when the last Lord Chancellor, Lord Cobbold, was asked to name a subject that could never be handled on stage, irrespective of the quality of writing and production, his reply was regicide', which goes to show how lucky Shakespeare was not to have been born in the enlightened twentieth century! Nevertheless, sex is what has concerned most guardians of our morality, and they must be surprised that all these years later we haven't suffered a surfeit of writhing naked bodies copulating on stage.

Since we are concerned with the written word which may just as easily be spoken, we should also look briefly at theatre censorship. The power given to the censor in 1737 was extended by the Theatre Act of 1843, which stipulated that the Lord Chamberlain must see everything in advance, enabling him to ban 'whenever he shall be of the opinion that it is fitting for the Preservation of Good Manners, Decorum, or for the Public Peace'. Yet incredibly, Lord Chamberlains were given no guidelines, were answerable to no one (except the monarch), and brought no qualifications to the job, except, it goes without saying, an abundance of good breeding.

In his article 'The Royal Smut Hound', written in 1965 and reprinted in *A View of the English Stage*, the critic Kenneth Tynan used the banning just before World War I of Sophocles' *Oedipus Rex* as an example of the Lord Chamberlain's stupidity, 'a baleful deterrent lurking on the threshold of creativity'. He quotes from a letter of protest written by the playwright Henry Arthur Jones (1851–1929), now little remembered but ranked alongside Pinero and Shaw by *The Oxford Companion to the Theatre*. In his complaint, Jones wrote to the Lord Chamberlain:

> Now, of course, if any considerable body of Englishmen are arranging to marry their mothers, whether by accident or design, it must be stopped at once. But it is not a frequent occurrence in any

class of English society. Throughout the course of my life I have not met more than six men who were anxious to do it.

Hilarious examples of changes demanded by the Lord Chamberlain would fill a book in their own right, but even in the so-called 'swinging sixties' authors were being instructed:

> For 'wind from a duck's behind', substitute 'wind from Mount Zion'. Omit 'piss off, piss off, piss off', substitute 'shut your steaming gob'. It is understood that wherever the word 'shit' appears, it will be altered in every case to 'it'.

To John Osborne, with whom the Lord Chamberlain conducted a running battle on almost every play, his instructions included:

> Delete 'menstrual periods'. [To which the director allegedly retorted that the words cut would block the flow of the scene.] (*Inadmissable Evidence*)
>
> Eliminate the line 'The tax man is almost definitely queer' [no substitute line referring to the Inspector of Taxes as a homosexual would be allowed]. (*The World of Paul Slickey*)
>
> The pause in the final line of '. . . Before I make a pass, I'll tell her the sun shines out of her – face' had to be taken out, or the whole couplet would have to be removed. (*The World of Paul Slickey*)

Among other changes forced on Osborne in various plays were 'muffin' for 'crumpet', 'urine' for 'piss', and in place of 'Leaping from the bridal bed, He preferred his youthful squire instead', the substitution of 'He preferred the companionship of his youthful squire instead'. Expressions like 'bridal bed' obviously had smuttier connotations to the ears of the Lord Chamberlain than implied homosexuality.

It has been said that great writers, like Henry Fielding, gave up the theatre for the freedom of the printed page, yet today the author and publisher face sniper-fire from a dozen-and-one official watchdogs, as well as over-zealous individuals. In the United States, literary works are even more vulnerable, and prudery comes in a multiplicity of disguises, although with care and luck a writer can avoid certain minefields. There is, incidentally, much common ground (although each party would be horrified at the comparison) between the reactionaries of South Africa or some of the States of America's deep

South, and those of the Soviet Union. In matters other than political issues their tastes and attitudes are remarkably similar.

However, powerful organisations such as the Society for the Suppression of Vice and, later, the Catholic Office for Decent Literature (NODL) transcended state boundaries, and were so powerful for many years of this century, that most American publishers took the easy way out and either submitted manuscripts or at least consulted these bodies before publishing.

The post offices and customs departments in England and America have generally vied with each other for the honour of being the nation's major watchdog in matters of morals, and again it has been the United States that has suffered worse. Among the modern 'classics' banned by the US Post Office are Hemingway's *For Whom the Bell Tolls*, Erskine Caldwell's *God's Little Acre* and *Tobacco Road* (which, as a play, had the longest run in the history of the American theatre), Alberto Moravia's *The Woman of Rome*, John O'Hara's *Appointment in Samarra* and James Jones' *From Here to Eternity*. Indeed, any respected author is vulnerable to the idiosyncratic whims of these watchdogs. One such eminent novelist was James Branch Cabell (1879–1958), whose *Jurgen* (1919) is a fascinating mixture of Arthurian legend and romance and Rabelaisian philosophy. Hugh Walpole, in his introduction to the English edition in 1921, said of it:

> I know no book in the English language that colours one's imagination and fancy quite as this one does – some more, some less, but no other in quite this way. The world of *Jurgen* with its grotesquerie, its sudden beauty, its poverty and its pity, its adventure and romance, is a world descended from earlier worlds, but unique in its own period.

As an enthusiast for Arthurian-style mythology, I'm inclined to agree with him; a couple of extracts later in the book illustrate Cabell's admirable style of storytelling.

Ironically, the Society for the Suppression of Vice might never have heard of the book had it not been for an astute theatrical press agent who needed only to read the beginning (in which Jurgen is given a magic shirt that makes him irresistible to women) to realise it presented a superb publicity gimmick for his show. He 'fed' a friendly newspaper columnist (the famous Heywood Brown) with the news that his chorus girls were busy reading the book in their spare moments to see who could collect the greatest number of 'dirty' passages. When the piece was published, the Society sprang into action, and an awed magistrate promptly banned the book, ordering the publisher to withdraw copies. Unfortunately, it was not until a couple of years later that sanity was restored by a trial at which the judge advised the jury to find the book acceptable in law.

In the United Kingdom, the record-breaking theatre comedy *No Sex Please, We're British*, epitomises our obsessive yet rather superficial interest in the subject. From the very earliest times interference by Church and Royalty in such matters has been more often concerned with blasphemy than with sex. When Elizabeth I saw a pamphlet written by John Stubbs advising her not to marry a French prince, she was so shocked by his effrontery that she ordered his right hand be cut off; but if she considered the punishment fitted the crime, it is highly unlikely that our Virgin Queen would ever have contemplated punishing the purveyor of pornography in such a fitting manner.

Each of those four 'milestones' in this century's erotica is very different, indeed, the only apparent common feature is the search by the central character for love and, in differing degrees, for sexual fulfilment. Radclyffe Hall, D. H. Lawrence and their most famous titles have been discussed and assessed at length by literary pundits better qualified than I. But personally, while finding both books overlong and even boring in places, I like them. What they have in common is a tremendous honesty that makes the reader *care* what happens. In the first instance this is because Radclyffe Hall demands from us a better understanding of the plight of the central character. Attitudes towards sexual relationships in all *four* books are very different, however, as the extracts chosen demonstrate.

The dictionary definition of an emotive word like 'obscene' is open to a variety of interpretations; obviously, what is 'obscene' to one person is not to another. The most common association is probably with the adjectives 'disgusting' and 'filthy', and it is usually applied to language. Yet there are those who believe that a *theme* dealing with a minority viewpoint on a moral issue is equally likely to upset the susceptibilities of 'decent' people. In this context, the most publicised 'obscene' book of the century, *The Well of Loneliness*, is by current moral standards an innocuous, somewhat overlong (512 pages) novel of limited literary pretensions – *without a single paragraph or even phrase calculated to arouse or excite, let alone shock.*

Loneliness is the theme in a poignant study of a beautiful but isolated young person craving understanding and affection, and of her efforts to relate to the people around her in a society unprepared to recognise her handicap. Even later, as a successful writer, she remains reserved and unable to communicate in personal relationships, and her love affairs are desperately intense. The author's 'crime' was that these affairs were with women, and in 1928 lesbianism (the defence preferred the word 'inversion' as opposed to 'perversion') was closely associated with obscenity.

The book and not the author went on trial; Radclyffe Hall was not even allowed to speak in its defence. What her critics could never forgive was her portrayal of 'evil perverts' as ordinary, otherwise 'respectable' women. The honour of womanhood sustained a particularly reprehensible slur in chapters dealing with World War I and the role of women ambulance drivers, although Radclyffe Hall (*c*1886–1943), herself a lesbian, had based the episode on personal experience and had displayed considerable courage in action in France. Her only 'sin' in most people's eyes today is the earnestness about which I complained earlier; she wrote of love in the gentlest sense and was never aggressive in making points that were deeply important to her.

Although its relationship to erotica is debatable, *The Well of Loneliness* has had such an impact on the laws relating to obscenity that the background to its publication is worth attention. The only biography of Radclyffe Hall, published a couple of years after her death, was written by a lifelong companion, Una Troubridge, and is more an affectionate reminiscence than a serious study. Little is known of her childhood, except that she was the only child of incompatible parents – a self-centred American mother, uninterested in her daughter, and an affectionate but irresponsible father, who was

---

(Opposite page) A title-page and frontispiece from *The Exquisite*. William Dugdale, one of the most successful 19th-century publishers of erotica and pornography, found a wide audience for this book in 1842–44. Despite the restrained style of this, he preferred to hide behind the pseudonym of H. Smith *(British Library)*

LANGUISHING MOMENTS

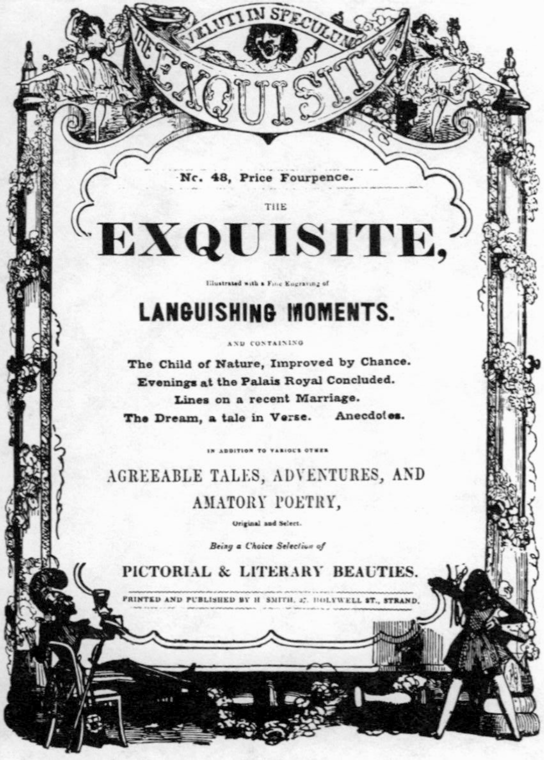

Nc. 48, Price Fourpence.

THE

EXQUISITE,

Illustrated with a Fine Engraving of

LANGUISHING MOMENTS.

AND CONTAINING

The Child of Nature, Improved by Chance.
Evenings at the Palais Royal Concluded.
Lines on a recent Marriage.
The Dream, a tale in Verse. Anecdotes.

IN ADDITION TO VARIOUS OTHER

AGREEABLE TALES, ADVENTURES, AND
AMATORY POETRY,

Original and Select.

Being a Choice Selection of

PICTORIAL & LITERARY BEAUTIES.

PRINTED AND PUBLISHED BY H. SMITH, 37, HOLYWELL ST., STRAND.

seldom around until the period leading up to his death, when she was eighteen. With this unfortunate background, it was small wonder that the only child, christened Marguerite, should be called 'Peter', and finally answer to 'John'. (The pen name was borrowed from her father, Radclyffe Radclyffe Hall.)

Further cushioned, and therefore isolated, by an affluent environment, the child was brought up by a well-meaning but ineffectual grandmother and, not surprisingly, her education was haphazard. Apart from showing some talent for music, she drifted aimlessly through her teens, twenties and early thirties, clutching at straws of affection from a number of women. Her early writing, a handful of interesting poems and short stories, was characteristic of that period in her life – intermittent flashes of talent, but undisciplined – and she had little interest in applying herself. When William Heinemann, the publisher, impressed with a short story, asked her to go away and write a full-length work – a thrill and inspiration for almost any writer – she was too lazy. However, encouraged by one of the genuine loves of her life, an influential older woman who recognised her talent, she began to persevere, and in 1924 her first novels *The Forge* and *The Unlit Lamp*, were published by Arrowsmith. However, recognition as a novelist came two years later when Cassell published *Adam's Breed* (1926), a poignant story (melodramatic, by today's more cynical standards) of an Italian waiter unable to come to terms with the harsher realities of life.

Whatever we may think of it today, *Adam's Breed* had merit, winning the Femina Vie Heureuse Prize 1925–6, and the James Tait Black Memorial Book Prize 1926. It was described by Newman Flower of Cassell (*see* Vera Brittain's *Radclyffe Hall, a Case of Obscenity?*) as the finest story he had been offered in twenty years, although he was not optimistic over sales. Yet 27,000 copies were bought in the first three weeks. Subsequent books, *The Master of the House* (1932) and *The Sixth Beatitude* (1936), were also sensitive

---

(Opposite page) Aristophanes' *Lysistrata* was illustrated in 1896 with eight drawings by Aubrey Beardsley (1872–98), for an edition privately published by Leonard Smithers. When he was dying two years later, Beardsley asked for the set to be destroyed, but fortunately they were not. Apart from his skill as an artist, he captured the *spirit* of this classic comedy – the enormous phallus, for example, in this scene, 'Cinesias Entreating Myrrhina to Coition'

treatments of rather uncommercial subjects, but would probably have been forgotten had it not been for the notoriety of *The Well of Loneliness*, which in turn might have sunk without trace had it not been for the trial that brought it to the attention of a much wider international audience than would have been expected. Over the past half-century, more than half a million copies have been sold, although many in pirate editions which of course did not benefit the author.

Radclyffe Hall showed courage in consciously tackling a subject she realised might provoke a storm of criticism and abuse, but she felt an obligation to speak out on behalf of a minority which had no other voice. At a time when the various 'gay' movements have been broadly accepted, it seems strange that such apprehension existed (yet this was after all 'the love that dare not speak its name'). *The Well of Loneliness* tells the story, partly autobiographical, of a wealthy girl 'Stephen', so christened because her parents had wanted a son. Lonely and intense, the child realises there is something different about her when she is shocked and revolted by a sudden declaration of passionate love from a pleasant young man, the first young person for whom she had felt a strong affection. Her concept of 'love' at this point was spiritual, but eventually she embarks on a series of homosexual affairs; these culminate in tragedy when the woman with whom she lives proves to be heterosexual and falls in love with Stephen's first male suitor, who has reappeared on the scene.

Cape published the book in 1928 to generally favourable reviews, and the storm did not break until an outraged editorial appeared in the *Sunday Express* of 19 August, demanding that the work be suppressed. 'Outrage' was the word used by the paper's editor, James Douglas. Commenting on a foreword by Havelock Ellis, a pioneer of sexual knowledge and understanding, which praised the book as possessing (apart from literary merit) 'notable psychological and sociological significance', Mr Douglas referred to such a defence and justification as 'an intolerable outrage – the first outrage of the kind in the annals of English fiction'.

He proceeded to get very hot under the collar when castigating sexual inversions and perversions.

> . . . this pestilence is devastating the younger generation. It is wrecking young lives. It is defiling young souls.

> I have seen the plague stalking shamelessly through great social assemblies. I have heard it whispered about by young men and women who do not and cannot grasp its unutterable putrefaction. Both aspects of it are thrust upon healthy and innocent minds. The contagion cannot be escaped. It pervades our social life.
>
> Perhaps it is a blessing in disguise or a curse in disguise that this novel forces upon our society a disagreeable task which it has hitherto shirked, the task of cleaning itself from the leprosy of these lepers, and making the air clean and wholesome once more.
>
> . . . I would rather give a healthy boy or a healthy girl a phial of prussic acid than this novel. Poison kills the body, but moral poison kills the soul.

Mr Douglas concluded by appealing to the literary world to 'keep its house in order'. It had not yet recovered, he maintained, from the harm done to it by the Oscar Wilde scandal.

Mr Douglas, apparently writing from the heart, was not the most original of journalists. The vitriolic analogy of dosing healthy youngsters with prussic acid was borrowed from a speech made over seventy years earlier by Lord Chief Justice Campbell when referring to what was, in the main, true pornography imported from the Continent. The relevant phrase used by Lord Campbell was 'a sale of poison more deadly than prussic acid, strychnine, or arsenic', but presumably the *Express* readers of the 1920s were not considered educated enough to take in all that.

Lord Campbell was the driving force in pushing through the Obscene Publications Act, 1857 (under which *The Well of Loneliness* was prosecuted) when he assured a dubious Parliament that:

> The measure was intended to apply *exclusively* [my italics] to works written for the single purpose of corrupting the morals of youth and of a nature calculated to shock the common feelings of decency in any well-regulated mind.

I suppose it is only fair to point out that Lord Campbell would have seen nothing inconsistent in that assurance, since he had a somewhat jaundiced view of literature and was most shocked by a recent import from France, *The Lady of the Camellias* (Alexandre Dumas, *fils*, 1848). In common with Douglas, it was the subject (in this case the story of a courtesan) and not the language that was offensive.

The melodramatic story of *The Lady of the Camellias* was tailor-made for nineteenth-century theatre, and self-appointed guardians of public morality were just as vigilant in their watch in this direction. The degree of outrage suffered by Mr Douglas in his role as champion of the Christian church was matched only by that of a Scottish clergyman whose thunderous but delightful broadside on the evils of the theatre came into my possession some years ago. Printed in 1819, it had the following title page:

THE STAGE
A Dangerous and Irreconcilable Enemy
to
CHRISTIANITY
Asserted and Proved in a letter
Addressed to a Comedian
By Valentine Ward, Minister, Aberdeen

The Rev. V. Ward prefixed his attack with this extract from James IV. 4: 'Ye adulterers and adultresses, know ye not that the friendship of the world is enmity with God? Whosoever, therefore, will be a friend of the world, is the enemy of God.' He also added a postscript, dated 27 November 1818 which starts:

> We are just informed by the public papers, that the Queen died on the 17th instant, and that the theatres were shut, and would remain so until further notice. But why shut the theatres, if the stage is innocent, good, and useful? Is there not in this conduct a tacit acknowledgement that the play-house is a bad place, and that people must have time to banish the thoughts of death from their minds, before they can go to it?

Today any publicity-minded theatrical producer or publisher would turn such outbursts to their advantage, knowing they were safe from interference from the law, but the publisher of *The Well of Loneliness*, Jonathan Cape, had made the mistake of sending a copy to the Home Secretary, Sir William Joynson-Hicks, a leading evangelist and the author of books on moral censorship! In November 1928 a prosecution was brought at Bow Street Magistrates' Court, where Sir Chartres Biron declared the book obscene, after refusing to hear forty defence witnesses who would have testified that in their opinion the book was *not* obscene and, indeed, had literary merit. Magistrates can apply either the letter or the spirit of the law, and Sir Chartres was within his rights in choosing the former since the case was tried under the Obscene Publications Act, 1857, which gives magistrates authority to order the destruction of 'any obscene publication held for sale or distribution on information laid before a court of summary jurisdiction'; in other words, evidence of literary merit was immaterial. (One of those literary figures who did not appear was George Bernard Shaw, who was sympathetic but excused himself on the grounds that he was himself immoral!)

The following month an appeal failed, and an order was made for the book to be destroyed. It was published in the United States and in 1929 prosecuted in much the same manner as the English edition. However, after listening to a number of witnesses, a special appeals court declared the book not to be obscene, and allowed it to go back on sale.

What then, in *The Well of Loneliness*, could have upset so many people? Take the heroine's first physical association with another woman, the spoilt, superficially attractive Angela Crosby. The development of the relationship is hardly erotic yet is heightened by an undercurrent of excitement.

> ... They walked on in silence while the light changed and deepened, growing always more golden and yet more elusive. And the birds, who loved that strange light, sang singly and then all together: 'We're happy, Stephen!'
>
> And turning to Angela, Stephen answered the birds: 'Your being here makes me so happy.'
>
> 'If that's true, why are you so shy of my name?'
>
> 'Angela–' mumbled Stephen.
>
> Then Angela said: 'It's just over three weeks since we met – how quickly our friendship's happened. I suppose it was meant, I believe in Kismet. You were awfully scared that first day at The Grange; why were you so scared?'
>
> Stephen answered slowly: 'I'm frightened now – I'm frightened of you.'
>
> 'Yet you're stronger than I am—'
>
> 'Yes, that's why I'm so frightened, you make me feel strong – do you want to do that?'
>
> 'Well – perhaps – you're so very unusual, Stephen.'

'Am I?'

'Of course, don't you know that you are? Why, you're altogether different from other people.'

Stephen trembled a little: 'Do you mind?' she faltered.

'I know that you're you,' teased Angela, smiling again, but she reached out and took Stephen's hand.

Something in the queer, vital strength of that hand stirred her deeply, so that she tightened her fingers: 'What in the Lord's name are you?' she murmered.

'I don't know. Go on holding like that to my hand – hold it tighter – I like the feel of your fingers.'

'Stephen, don't be absurd!'

'Go on holding my hand, I like the feel of your fingers.'

'Stephen, you're hurting, you're crushing my rings!'

And now they were under the trees by the lakes, their feet falling softly on the luminous carpet. Hand in hand they entered that place of deep stillness, and only their breathing disturbed the stillness for a moment, then it folded back over their breathing.

'Look,' said Stephen, and she pointed to the swan called Peter, who had come drifting past on his own white reflection. 'Look,' she said, 'this is Morton, all beauty and peace – it drifts like that swan does, on calm, deep water. And all this beauty and peace is for you, because now you're part of Morton.'

Angela said: 'I've never known peace, it's not in me – I don't think I'll find it here, Stephen.' And as she spoke she released her hand, moving a little away from the girl.

But Stephen continued to talk on gently; her voice sounded almost like that of a dreamer: 'Lovely, oh lovely it is, our Morton. On evenings in winter these lakes are quite frozen, and the ice looks like slabs of gold in the sunset, when you and I come and stand here in the winter. And as we walk back we can smell the log fires long before we can see them, and we love that good smell because it means home, and our home is Morton – and we're happy, happy – we're utterly contented and at peace, we're filled with the peace of this place—'

'Stephen – don't.'

'We're both filled with the old peace of Morton, because we love each other so deeply – and because we're perfect, a perfect thing, you and I – not two separate people but one. And our love has lit a great comforting beacon, so that we need never be afraid of the dark any more – we can warm ourselves at our love, we can

> lie down together, and my arms will be round you—'
>
> She broke off abruptly, and they stared at each other.
>
> 'Do you know what you're saying?' Angela whispered.
>
> And Stephen answered: 'I know that I love you, and that nothing else matters in the world.'
>
> Then, perhaps because of that glamorous evening, with its spirit of queer, unearthly adventure, with its surge to strange, unendurable sweetness, Angela moved a step nearer to Stephen, then another, until their hands were touching. And all that she was, and all that she had been and would be again, perhaps even tomorrow, was fused at that moment into one mighty impulse, one imperative need, and that need was Stephen. Stephen's need was now here, by sheer force of its blind and uncomprehending will to appeasement.
>
> Then Stephen took Angela in to her arms, and she kissed her full on the lips, as a lover.
>
> Later, jealous of Angela, Stephen demands:
>
> 'Was it all a mistake? Is there no one between us except your husband? Angela, look at me – I will have the truth.'
>
> For answer Angela kissed her.
>
> Stephen's strong but unhappy arms went round her, and suddenly stretching out her hand, she switched off the little lamp on the table, so that the room was lit only by firelight. They could not see each other's faces very clearly any more, because there was only firelight. And Stephen spoke such words as a lover will speak when his heart is burdened to breaking; when his doubts must bow down and be swept away before the unruly flood of his passion. There in that shadowy, firelit room, she spoke such words as lovers have spoken ever since the divine, sweet madness of God flung the thought of love into Creation.

The following narrative sums up the frustration of a lesbian in an intolerant society. Stephen's affair with the feckless Angela is disintegrating:

> That night she [Stephen] stared at herself in the glass; and even as she did so she hated her body with its muscular shoulders, its small compact breasts, and its slender flanks of an athlete. All her life she must drag this body of hers like a monstrous fetter imposed on her spirit. This strangely ardent yet sterile body that must worship yet

> never be worshipped in return by the creature of its adoration. She longed to maim it, for it made her feel cruel; it was so white, so strong and so self-sufficient; yet withal so poor and unhappy a thing that her eyes filled with tears and her hate turned to pity. She began to grieve over it, touching her breasts with pitiful fingers, stroking her shoulders, letting her hands slip along her straight thighs – Oh, poor and most desolate body!

However, lest it be construed that I am loading the dice, let's return to the effect on a novel's career of so-called obscene *language*. Thirty-two years after it was first published, D. H. Lawrence's *Lady Chatterley's Lover* incurred the full wrath of the law when, in 1960, the very respectable Penguin Books introduced the unexpurgated version in paperback. The trial – the first prosecution under a recently passed Obscene Publications Act – was another milestone in the history of English literature, but the solemnity of one passage in the opening address to the jury from Mr Griffith-Jones, senior Treasury Counsel leading for the prosecution, added an element of high farce, so I might be forgiven for using it slightly out of context. Meaning no disrespect to Mr Griffith-Jones, try to imagine *any* senior representative of the law, recognised for his oratory, eloquence and dignity, having to wrap his tongue around the following:

> . . . but words – no doubt they will be said to be good old Anglo-Saxon four-letter words, and no doubt they are – appear again and again. These matters are not voiced normally in this court, but when it forms the whole subject matter of the prosecution, then, members of the jury, we cannot avoid voicing them. The word 'fuck' or 'fucking' occurs no less than thirty times. I have added them up, but I do not guarantee that I have added them all up [Author's note: If you disagree with this addition please do not write to me!] 'Cunt' fourteen times; 'balls' thirteen times; 'shit' and 'arse' six times apiece; 'cock' four times; 'piss' three times . . .

All this is a far cry from Radclyffe Hall's somewhat genteel style. Yet it is not the explicit language that makes passages in the book erotic – far from it; it is Lawrence's own evocative style of narrative. The obscene words can be removed without diluting the vivid colours he paints and no one in his right mind could accuse him of using them for effect, as we will see.

3

Authors in Erotic Mood

Several of the novels of D. H. Lawrence (1885–1930) contain passages that, when taken in context, are erotic. Whether the reader merely has his (or her) sense of sexual awareness heightened or whether underclothes become uncomfortably tight, few can read Lawrence's descriptions of sexual passion with indifference. It has been said that Lawrence had an 'unhealthy' preoccupation with sex, but even those critics would concede that he was a powerful and sensitive writer. It is this sensitivity, this honesty, that produces erotica of the highest quality. When you stop to think about it, the act of coitus is a physical action not far removed from many athletic sports (I've forgotten the formula, apart from the basic equation: 1 orgasm = 1 × 5-mile run). As such, one would assume there are a limited number of things we can say about it. Yet true eroticism is seldom boring, unlike the pornographic equivalent which invariably is, because it might have been served up by computer.

Lady Chatterley's Lover (1928) is the title that brought Lawrence to the notice of audiences outside the relatively small literary circles, yet it is not considered his best work, or even the most erotic. For collectors, the book to go for is *The Rainbow* (Methuen, 1915), which was not only banned but had 1,011 copies destroyed by order of the magistrate, so that if you're lucky enough to come across one of the handful of first-edition copies that still exists, I know a number of dealers and collectors who would pay several hundred pounds (£) for it. Another overlong (200,000 words) study in passionate relationships, and in the country setting Lawrence knew so well, the story of *The Rainbow* concerns the Brangwen family, and particularly Tom a farmer, his step-daughter Anna and her child Ursula, and judging from the expurgated edition the original love scenes must have been very erotic. Having spent three years of his life on it, he remained bitter about what he described as the 'capitulation' of his publishers without a fight. The foreword to *A Bibliography of the Writings of D. H. Lawrence* by Edward D. McDonald, asserts that his publisher 'almost wept' before the magistrate, claiming he had been misadvised by his reader! Yet Lawrence, with a coal-miner father and schoolteacher mother, was strangely intolerant of erotica that did not conform to his own moral code – sexual union through love – and publicly attacked other authors whose works did not meet his approval.

However, what no one would deny were Lawrence's honesty and, for the most part, his command of language. Even people who have not read *Lady Chatterley's Lover* may know in outline the story of Connie, the young wife of Sir Clifford Chatterley, wounded in the war and now paralysed from the waist down, of her superficial relationship with the writer, Michaelis, and of her love affair with Mellors, the gamekeeper on her husband's estate.

Lawrence, long before drawing attention to her sexual abstinence, establishes Connie's *isolation* in what is ostensibly a normal, happy home. One notices the similarity with Radclyffe Hall's heroine, who was made to feel different because of her subconscious homosexual inclinations. Connie Chatterley's isolation also stems from the absence of common ground: the lack of a cultural meeting point between her, her aristocratic husband and his family, although there is, initially, a purely aesthetic bond with Sir Clifford.

To me, Lawrence is at his best in setting the mood before Connie breaks the traces:

> Time went on. Whatever happened, nothing happened, because she was so beautifully out of contact. She and Clifford lived in their ideas and his books. She entertained . . . there were always people in the house. Time went on as the clock does, half past eight instead of half past seven.

Some of the eminent literary figures called at the trial to testify on behalf of Lawrence were cross-examined thoroughly by Mr Griffith-Jones. Opinion cannot be represented as fact, and its power to influence should be related directly to how much it can be supported by reasonable evidence. We form our judgements on what we regard as the validity of the opinion or on the weight of the evidence. Yet often Lawrence's prose style provides its own best defence. In the passage below a prosecution suggestion that the *repetition* of words is unnecessary and therefore not good writing is refuted by our senses. The scene in which Connie meets Mellors outdoors, shortly after they have become lovers, is surely both erotic and beautiful?

> He led her through the wall of prickly trees, that were difficult to come through, to a place where was a little space and a pile of dead boughs. He threw one or two dry ones down, put his coat and waistcoat over them, and she had to lie down there under the boughs of the tree, like an animal, while he waited, standing there in his shirt and breeches, watching her with haunted eyes. But still he was provident – he made her lie properly, properly. Yet he broke the band of her underclothes, for she did not help him, only lay inert.
>
> He too had bared the front part of his body and she felt his naked flesh against her as he came into her. For a moment he was still inside her, turgid there and quivering. Then as he began to move, in the sudden helpless orgasm, there awoke in her new strange thrills rippling inside her. Rippling, rippling, rippling, like a flapping overlapping of soft flames, soft as feathers, running to points of brilliance, exquisite, exquisite and melting her all molten inside. It was like bells rippling up and up to a culmination. She lay unconscious of the wild little cries she uttered at the last. But it was over too soon, too soon, and she could no longer force her own conclusion with her own activity. This was different, different. She could do nothing. She could no longer harden and grip for her own satisfaction upon him. She could only wait, wait and moan in spirit as she felt him withdrawing, withdrawing and contracting, coming to the terrible moment when he would slip out of her and be gone. Whilst all her womb was open and soft, and softly clamouring, like a sea-anemone under the tide, clamouring for him to come in again and make a fulfilment for her. She clung to him unconscious in passion, and he never quite slipped from her, and she felt the soft bud of him within her stirring, and strange rhythms flushing up into her with a strange rhythmic growing motion, swelling and swelling till it filled all her cleaving consciousness, and then began again the unspeakable motion that was not really motion, but pure deepening whirlpools of sensation swirling deeper and deeper through all her tissue and consciousness, till she was one perfect concentric fluid of feeling, and she lay there crying

> in unconscious inarticulate cries. The voice out of the uttermost night, the life! The man heard it beneath him with a kind of awe, as his life sprang out into her. And as it subsided, he subsided too and lay utterly still, unknowing, while her grip on him slowly relaxed, and she lay inert. And they lay and knew nothing, not even of each other, both lost. Till at last he began to rouse and become aware of his defenceless nakedness, and she was aware that his body was loosening its clasp on her. He was coming apart; but in her breast she felt she could not bear him to leave her uncovered. He must cover her now for ever.

Lawrence's strength lay in his ability to uncover the very soul of his characters. Connie emerges from the limbo that had insulated her from a deteriorating marriage, headlong into a brief and unsatisfactory affair with the writer Michaelis. But it is not to him as a person she is attracted; it is what he represents at that moment, and in terms of love their relationship is a compromise.

With Mellors, the man she grew to love, there was no pretence; the remaining barriers of reserve being torn down one by one. The use of repetition criticised by the prosecution as inadequacy on the part of the writer was effective, particularly in the analogy between a heaving ocean and a woman in the throes of ecstasy.

> She quivered again at the potent inexorable entry inside her, so strange and terrible. It might come with the thrust of a sword in her softly-opened body, and that would be death. She clung in a sudden anguish of terror. But it came with a strange slow thrust of peace, the dark thrust of peace and a ponderous, primordial tenderness, such as made the world in the beginning. And her terror subsided in her breast, her breast dared to be gone in peace, she held nothing. She dared to let go everything, all herself, and be gone to the flood.
>
> And it seemed she was like the sea, nothing but dark waves rising and heaving, heaving with a great swell, so that slowly her whole darkness was in motion, and she was ocean rolling its dark, dumb mass. Oh, and far down inside her the deeps parted and rolled asunder, in long, far-travelling billows, and ever, at the quick of her, the depths parted and rolled asunder, from the centre of soft plunging, as the plunger went deeper and deeper, touching lower, and she was deeper and deeper and deeper disclosed, the heavier the billows of her rolled away to some shore, uncovering her, and

> closer and closer plunged the palpable unknown, and further and further rolled the waves of herself away from herself, leaving her, till suddenly, in a soft, shuddering convulsion, the quick of all her plasm was touched, she knew herself touched, the consummation was upon her, and she was gone. She was gone, she was not, and she was born: a woman . . .

Mellors is a complex person, with little formal education but a natural ability that had earned him a commission in the Army. He can speak 'ordinary' English, but reverts to local dialect almost belligerently when unsure of himself, when he feels vulnerable to aggression or even love:

> He dropped the shirt and stood still looking towards her. The sun through the low window sent in a beam that lit up his thighs and slim belly and the erect phallus rising darkish and hot-looking from the little cloud of vivid gold-red hair. She was startled and afraid.
>
> 'How strange!' she said slowly. 'How strange he stands there! So big! and so dark and cock-sure! Is he like that?
>
> The man looked down the front of his slender white body, and laughed. Between the slim breasts the hair was dark, almost black. But at the root of the belly, where the phallus rose thick and arching, it was gold-red, vivid in a little cloud.
>
> 'So proud!' she murmured, uneasy. 'And so lordly! Now I know why men are so overbearing! But he's lovely, really. Like another being! A bit terrifying! But lovely really! And he comes to me!—' She caught her lower lip between her teeth, in fear and excitement.
>
> The man looked down in silence at the tense phallus, that did not change. – 'Ay!' he said at last, in a little voice. 'Ay ma lad! tha're theer right enough. Yi, tha mun rear thy head! Theer on thy own, eh? an' ta'es no count o' nob'dy! Tha ma'es nowt o' me, John Thomas. Art boss? of me? Eh well, tha're more cocky than me, an' tha says less. John Thomas! Dost want her? Dost want my lady Jane? Tha's dipped me in again, tha hast. Ay, an' tha comes up smilin'. – Ax'er then! Ax lady Jane! Say: Lift up your heads o' ye gates, that the king of glory may come in. Ay, th' cheek on thee! Cunt, that's what tha're after. Tell lady Jane tha wants cunt. John Thomas, an' th' cunt o' lady Jane!—'
>
> 'Oh, don't tease him,' said Connie, crawling on her knees on the bed towards him and putting her arms round his white slender

loins, and drawing him to her so that her hanging, swinging breasts touched the tip of the stirring, erect phallus, and caught the drop of moisture. She held the man fast.

'Lie down!' he said. 'Lie down! Let me come!'

He was in a hurry now.

And afterwards, when they had been quite still, the woman had to uncover the man again, to look at the mystery of the phallus.

'And now he's tiny, and soft like a little bud of life!' she said, taking the soft small penis in her hand. 'Isn't he somehow lovely! so on his own, so strange! And so innocent! And he comes so far into me! You must never insult him, you know. He's mine too. He's not only yours. He's mine. And so lovely and innocent!' And she held the penis soft in her hand.

He laughed.

'Blest be the tie that binds our hearts in kindred love,' he said.

If learned counsel had managed to count the number of times that 'fuck' and 'cunt' appeared in *Lady Chatterley*, he certainly couldn't have managed to keep tabs on Henry Miller (1891–1980) without a pocket calculator. Most people wouldn't identify Miller with erotica, thinking of him as a writer of dirty books, recalling perhaps two or three titles vaguely something to do with the tropics . . . and there they wouldn't be far wrong, since much of his work is dazzling in its heat and colour. His work has been compared with James Joyce's, particularly *Ulysses*, but if Miller's style is crazy in the eyes of the uninitiated, then at least he has moments of rationality, and at those times he can be very erotic.

Indeed, though not awarded the serious respectability of (say) Lawrence (in literary, not drawing-room, terms) Miller has always been highly regarded by other writers. He began writing in his late thirties and his output has been prolific; when Jay Martin embarked on an unauthorised biography, *Always Merry and Bright, The Life of Henry Miller*, he had to work his way through 100,000 manuscripts, housed in twenty-three libraries.

Miller did not find his feet as a writer – leading a stranger-than-fiction vagabond existence in New York and Paris, recaptured in the autobiographical *Tropics* – until he was almost forty. He contributed a number of articles to a Paris literary journal in the years leading up to World War II, when many great American authors made Paris their home. By the time *Tropic of Cancer* was published in 1934, he was still living on the breadline, being financially supported by the writer Anaïs Nin. *Cancer* turned him into a literary lion overnight. (Coincidentally, the book was compared very favourably by T. S. Eliot with *Lady Chatterley's Lover.*) *Black Spring* was his next book following in the same.pattern, a fictionalised confessional fantasy, and *Tropic of Capricorn* came in 1939. Shortly afterwards, George Orwell added his praise to that of most of his contemporaries, describing Miller as 'the only imaginative prose-writer among the English speaking races for some years past'. The *Tropics* were not published in England or the United States for another quarter of a century. When Grove Press, the American publishing house, published *Cancer* in 1961, the foreword described Miller as 'the greatest living writer', but this did not stop it being banned two years later, although the New York court's decision was close (4–3).

With the threat of Nazi invasion Miller left France for Greece before returning to the United States, settling in California – where he eventually died – a very different world from his native Brooklyn. From then on, as part of America's literary establishment, he became more and more the guru to whom younger writers turned for inspiration, although he appeared to lose interest in post-war society, and ironically its decadence. His own life, mirrored in the *Tropics*, seems incredibly decadent to the outsider, nearly fifty years later, but he didn't see it that way. *Cancer*, dealing with his long spell in Paris, came first and, in the sense that it was used to test the courts in 1963, might be regarded as the spearhead. (The US Supreme Court overruled the New York decision a year later.) But *Capricorn*, originally published five years later yet dealing with his youth and early jobs, is in some ways a more complete book, and I have used this to illustrate Miller's apparent obsession with sex and his remarkably graphic style.

In the following extract, the young would-be writer, desperately ducking the challenge of actually sitting down to write, diverts his thoughts from reality, and daydreams thus:

> Standing knee-deep in the lava beds and my eyes choked with sperm: J. P. Morganana is placidly wiping his ass while the telephone girls plug the switchboards, while dicks with rubber

hoses practice the third degree, while my old friend MacGregor scrubs the germs out of his cock and sweetens it and examines it under the microscope. Everybody is caught with his pants down, including the strip teasers who wear no pants, no beards, no moustaches, just a little patch to cover their twinkling little cunts. Sister Antolina lying in the convent bed, her guts trussed up, her arms akimbo and waiting for the Resurrection, waiting, waiting for life without hernia, without intercourse, without sin, without evil, meanwhile nibbling a few animal crackers, a pimento, some fancy olives, a little head cheese. The Jew-boys on the East Side, in Harlem, the Bronx, Carnarsie, Bronville, opening and closing the trapdoors, pulling out arms and legs, turning the sausage machine, clogging up the drains, working like fury for cash down and if you let a peep out of you out you go. With eleven hundred tickets in my pocket and a Rolls Royce waiting for me downstairs I could have the most excruciatingly marvellous time, throwing a fuck into each and everyone respectively regardless of age, sex, race, religion, nationality, birth or breeding . . .

This is the incarnation of the hallucination of sex, the sea nymph squirming in the maniac's arms. I watch the two of them as they move spasmodically inch by inch around the floor: they move like an octopus working up a rut. Between the dangling tentacles the music shimmers and flashes, now breaks in a cascade of sperm and rose water, forms again into an oily spout, a column erect without feet, collapses again like chalk, leaving the upper part of the leg phosphorescent, a zebra standing in a pool of golden marshmallow, one leg striped, the other molten. A golden marshmallow octopus with rubber hinges and molten hooves, its sex undone and twisted into a knot. On the sea floor the oysters are doing the St Vitus dance, some with lockjaw, some with double-jointed knees.

However, when it came to sex – his own sex life – Miller is usually more coherent, applying a form of discipline born of single-mindedness. The following is typical of his philosophy as a young man:

Well, all this is simply by way of leading up to the general sexual confusion which prevailed at this time. It was like taking a flat in the Land of Fuck. The girl upstairs, for instance . . . she used to come down now and then, when the wife was giving a recital, to

Thomas Rowlandson (1756–1827), one of Britain's best-loved cartoonists, included a large number of 'indecent' drawings in his vast output. Perhaps the most delightful, and certainly typical of the artist's unique *joie de vivre*, were the posthumously published *Pretty Little Games for Young Girls and Gentlemen* (1845), with Rowlandson's own verse accompanying the ten plates. This is 'Rural Felicity or Love in a Chaise' (*Courtesy of Raymond O'Shea*)

THE
Life and Adventures
OF
FANNY HILL.
A Fair Cyprian,
BY JOHN. CLELAND.

Dugdale frequently threw pretence to the winds, and this little Dugdale edition of *Fanny Hill* has explicit hand-coloured illustrations. It is not well produced, but its rarity value makes it worth around £500 today (*Courtesy of Bosworth Books*)

look after the kid. She was so obviously a simpleton that I didn't give her any notice at first. But like all the others she had a cunt too, a sort of impersonal personal cunt which she was unconsciously conscious of. The oftener she came down the more conscious she got, in her unconscious way. One night, when she was in the bathroom, after she had been in there a suspiciously long while, she got me to thinking of things. I decided to take a peep through the key-hole and see for myself what was what. Lo and behold, if she isn't standing in front of the mirror stroking and petting her little pussy. Almost talking to it, she was. I was so excited I didn't know what to do first. I went back into the big room, turned out the lights, and lay there on the couch waiting for her to come out. As I lay there I could still see that bushy cunt of hers and the fingers strumming it like. I opened my fly to let my pecker twitch about in the cool of the dark, I tried to mesmerize her from the couch, or at least I tried letting my pecker mesmerize her. 'Come here, you bitch,' I kept saying to myself, 'come in here and spread that cunt over me.' She must have caught the message immediately, for in a jiffy she had opened the door and was groping about in the dark to find the couch. I didn't say a word, I didn't make a move. I just kept my mind riveted on her cunt moving quietly in the dark like a crab. Finally she was standing beside the couch. She didn't say a word either. She just stood there quietly and as I slid my hand up her legs she moved one foot a little to open her crotch a bit more. I don't think I ever put my hand into such a juicy crotch in all my life. It was like paste running down her legs, and if there had been any billboards handy I could have plastered up a dozen or more. After a few moments, just as naturally as a cow lowered its head to graze, she bent over and put it in her mouth. I had my whole four fingers inside her, whipping it up to a froth. Her mouth was stuffed full and the juice pouring down her legs. Not a word out of us, as I say. Just a couple of quiet maniacs working away in the dark like grave-diggers.

Undoubtedly parts of the book are pornographic in the sense that for long passages the flow of the story is interrupted by repetitive descriptions of the sex act and its permutations, apparently calculated to excite the reader. Yet I doubt whether thoughts about the reader ever entered the mind of Henry Miller; he probably wrote for himself. The most truly erotic sequence, in my opinion, partly because of his down-to-earth documentary style, is the following extract:

> One of the reasons why I never got anywhere with the bloody music is that it was always mixed up with sex. As soon as I was able to play a song the cunts were around me like flies. To begin with, it was largely Lola's fault. Lola was my first piano teacher Lola Niessen. It was a ridiculous name and typical of the neighbourhood we were living in then. It sounded like a stinking bloater, or a wormy cunt. To tell the truth, Lola was not exactly a beauty. She looked somewhat like a Kalmuck or a Chinook, with sallow complexion and bilious-looking eyes. She had a few warts and wens, not to speak of the moustache. What excited me, however, was her hairiness; she had wonderful long fine black hair which she arranged in ascending and descending buns on her Mongolian skull. At the nape of the neck she curled it up in a serpentine knot. She was always late in coming, being a conscientious idiot, and by the time she arrived I was always a bit enervated from masturbating . . .

The youthful Henry's dreams are eventually realised:

> I had a feeling sometimes that she knew I was following her and that she enjoyed it. I think she was waiting for me to waylay her – I think that was what she wanted. Anyway, one night I was lying in the grass near the railroad tracks; it was a sweltering summer's night and people were lying about anywhere and everywhere, like panting dogs. I wasn't thinking of Lola at all – I was just mooning there, too hot to think about anything. Suddenly I see a woman coming along the narrow cinderpath. I'm lying sprawled out on the embankment and nobody around that I can notice. The woman is coming along slowly, head down, as though she were dreaming. As she gets close I recognize her. 'Lola!' I call. 'Lola!' She seems to be really astonished to see me there. 'Why, what are you doing here?' she says, and with that she sits down beside me on the embankment. I didn't bother to answer her, I didn't say a word – I just crawled over her and flattened her. 'Not here, please,' she begged, but I paid no attention. I got my hand between her legs, all tangled up in that thick sporran of hers, and she was sopping wet, like a horse salivating. It was my first fuck, be Jesus, and it had to be that a train would come along and shower hot sparks over us. Lola was terrified. It was her first fuck too, I guess, and she probably needed it more than I, but when she felt the sparks she wanted to tear loose. It was like trying to hold down a wild mare. I

couldn't keep her down, no matter how I wrestled with her. She got up shook her clothes down, and adjusted the bun at the nape of her neck. 'You must go home,' she says. 'I'm not going home,' I said, and with that I took her by the arm and started walking. We walked along in dead silence for quite a distance. Neither of us seemed to be noticing where we were going. Finally we were out on the highway and up above us were the reservoirs and near the reservoirs was a pond. Instinctively I headed towards the pond. We had to pass under some low-hanging trees as we neared the pond. I was helping Lola to stoop down when suddenly she slipped, dragging me with her. She made no effort to get up; instead, she caught hold of me and pressed me to her, and to my complete amazement I also felt her slip her hand in my fly. She caressed me so wonderfully that in a jiffy I came in her hand. Then she took my hand and put it between her legs. She lay back completely relaxed and opened her legs wide. I bent over and kissed every hair on her cunt; I put my tongue in her navel and licked it clean. Then I lay with my head between her legs and lapped up the drool that was pouring from her. She was moaning now and clutching wildly with her hands; her hair had come completely undone and was lying over her bare abdomen. To make it short, I got it in again, and I held it a long time, for which she must have been damned grateful because she came I don't know how many times – it was like a pack of firecrackers going off, and with it all she sunk her teeth into me, bruised my lips, clawed me, ripped my shirt and what the hell not. I was branded like a steer when I got home and took a look at myself in the mirror.

The only thing Lawrence, Miller and Stanley Kauffmann (born 1916) had in common is that all spent some time in Europe, but there the comparison ends. Kauffmann enjoyed a conventional middle-class background, graduating from New York University, and emerging as a writer, after a period in the theatre where he acted and directed. One can pick up any one of his dozen or so plays and books – of which *The Philanderer* is the fourth novel – and know they will prove a pleasant experience. He is a highly skilled professional, not bothered with breaking new ground, but possessing the discipline seldom found in writers of so-called genius, not to indulge themselves in overwriting. His novels remind me of *cinéma-vérité* or the dramatised documentary; they portray a slice of life, without frills, but essentially real. Kauffmann is a writer concerned with the truth.

Kauffmann would be the first to admit that the trial in England (the book had been published unchallenged in the United States to favourable reviews) benefited his pocket considerably. But *The Philanderer* (did he realise, I wonder, that a play with this title was written by G. B. Shaw in 1893 and first performed in 1907?) merits a place in a history of erotica because it changed the law, making the courts from then on apply a little common sense to defining the word 'obscene'. The gist of Mr Justice Stable's summing up was that we cannot be influenced by the possibilities of corrupting a child, when contemplating publication of a serious novel for adults; and that without the 'corrupt and deprave' clause, it is not a criminal offence to shock or disgust one's readers.

Kauffmann's hero, Russell Conrad, is the philanderer of the title, an ordinary, basically decent young American advertising man with a compulsion for laying every passably attractive woman he encounters. In this respect he might symbolise the wish fulfilment of many other ordinary, basically decent men, young and old. But to Conrad, like someone addicted to alcohol or gambling, it is a disease and he has no control over his actions, despite an awareness of ultimate disaster, not least the inevitable destruction of his marriage to Madeleine, an actress with whom he believes he is much in love. Kauffmann's skill lies not only in his accurate observation of people and their relationships, but in making Conrad, despite his glaring faults and weaknesses, so sympathetic that the reader cares. One wills him to jump off the out-of-control vehicle gathering momentum downhill on its path to destruction.

Wayland Young in *Eros Denied* considers the book has sociological values, describing it as an 'instructive study of the masochistic temperament which must have a jailer'. He suggests that Conrad could have admitted to Madeleine that he lived in constant fear of her discovering his infidelities, in which case the marriage would either have broken up on the spot, or they would have come to some arrangement, whereby (in either situation) he would have been free to lay all and sundry. But freedom, Young suggests, is the one thing Conrad could not accept.

Conrad's character is established very early in the book with an almost over-the-shoulder glance at an affair that has ended before our hero is prepared for it. Like a juggler with half-a-dozen balls in the air, he is surprised when one ball appears to have a mind of its own. He can afford to be dispassionate, the girl means nothing to him, but his pride is hurt:

> She shrugged to indicate that she didn't care one way or another; time wasn't going to make any difference.
>
> He put on his coat and kissed her. She came into his arms like a patient to a doctor. He kissed her dead mouth and would have liked to spit at her.
>
> 'I'll call you next week,' he said soothingly, 'early. Maybe Monday, if I can.'
>
> 'If you want to,' she said. 'And look. Don't go sending me any more presents. I mean, that's just part of the whole thing. That's not going to change anything.'
>
> You scut, he thought. You scut, you slut, you scut. Think you're so smart. Think you've stripped the hide off me and can lay on with the lash . . .
>
> But the anger wasn't enough to thaw the panic.
>
> 'O.K. dear,' he agreed. 'Whatever you say. I'll call you Monday.'
>
> On the way home he consigned her to hell. Wrote her off. Good as finished. Anyway, what did he care about her? He knew where he would always be loved. What was she, after all? Just a dumb broad. Just a dumb bed-ridden broad. Ha. That was good.
>
> He'd proved his point with her. He'd conquered her, he'd dallied, he'd had the innermost fruit. . . .
>
> But to be cast out this way.
>
> And by a –God damn it, by a *girl*.

Conrad seduces the wife of an office colleague. He plans the operation clinically, all the time weakly promising himself that nothing will happen. His conscience puts up a token resistance, but it is out of its depth, having been on a hiding to nothing for years. Part of Conrad's vulnerability, and why we have a sneaking sympathy with him, is that he never takes anyone for granted, and with Clare he is as apprehensive as though this were his first affair:

> They sipped their drinks and talked, and it was clear to both of them, he thought, that this occasion was different from any other time they'd spent together. Before this they had been thoroughly

comfortable; the other night they had felt like old, old friends. But now there was constraint, the conversation came slowly, in little forced patches and this constraint only confirmed matters for him. She was as conscious as he was that they were alone; she knew, too, that tremendous matters impended.

And now there was nothing left in him but fear and desire. Fear that it was going to happen; desire for it to happen. Her presence, the nearness of that rich and complicated body, stung straight to the heart of his weakness and wiped away the last restraint, left him only with formless fear and desire. It was as if the warders he had posted had been frightened helpless, could only stand dumb and watch the prisoner escape . . . and had known that he would try to escape, so were doubly frightened at their helplessness.

'Well, I guess I ought to be going,' he said, putting down his glass. It was one last poor effort, but damn it, it would also bring things to a head.

'Sure,' she said at once, a phantom of reluctance speeding across her face. 'I suppose you have lots to do. Oh,' she said as if she had just remembered, 'you were asking about Frazee the other night. My home town.'

'Yes, that's right.'

'I meant to show you some pictures. But if you're in a hurry—'

Oh, lady, lady. I knew there'd be a last harpoon.

'Sure, I'd love to see them. Especially that man you told me about with the six toes on one foot and four on the other.'

She laughed and got some photographs from a desk in the corner. She handed them to him one by one, and he looked at them and asked questions and heard replies and he felt, as her hand came to him each time and as he caught clearly the scent of her cologne and of her hair, that he rushed to the precipice and the earth slanted down toward the edge.

Then the single photographs were finished and there was an album. He would have to sit next to her to look at that.

Oh, my God, no, let me go, he pleaded silently. Be bored. Be angry. Throw me out.

'Of course I do,' he said, and sat on the arm of the sofa beside her.

Now there was no hiding it. He could see her fingers tremble slightly as she turned the pages. He could hear the dry coda in her voice as her breath failed to last for any one sentence. Now as he leaned forward, her shoulder brushed his chest and with that touch his mind flew to a thousand fantastic images. Now he could see the division of her breasts, the small gold hairs above her lip, the roundness of her belly . . . there and there and there.

He could have them. He could have them. And this certainly made his throat tighten and his scalp tingle.

She turned the page and came to a picture of herself as a child. He saw that this was the occasion, the chance. He could laugh at that picture and kiss her hair, the side of her head. If he had misread her, he could pass the kiss off as simple affection; no harm done. If he was right. . . .

Hurry. . . .

'Ah,' he laughed at the picture of the barefoot child with lovely careless hair, with sun and health around her, 'you look like a visitor from the upper air.'

He kissed her temple. Depending on her reaction now, he would either pat her shoulder next, saying she was sweet, or . . .

She turned and looked at him. He knew it was over, hopeless.

There was the faint worried look on her brow. Her mouth started to say his name, then faltered. She drew in her breath in a short sharp sigh and came toward him. He bent forward to meet her and they kissed.

Her mouth found his with immediate warmth and disclosure. It was no mere kissing. She wanted him, she had thought of this, her blood burned. This was a woman, all of her, beginning with her mouth.

How her mouth enfolded his, how warm, how moist and tight, how salt-alive. Never . . . drowning . . . never . . .

Suddenly, with a little gasp, she pulled back, her mouth still partly open, and stared at him, her eyes filmed slightly, her breath short and quick.

She swallowed. 'Russell,' she said, almost questioningly. She was trying to invite, to apologize, to make sure, to back out, to explain and continue. She didn't know which to do first, and she halted after the ambiguous inflection of his name . . .

. . . And kissing her, he thought: This must lead somewhere. Not just two kids content to grapple on a sofa. She would despise me. Having gone this far, I must go further. Now any qualms and restraints were wiped away, completely forgotten. He had only desire for her and an odd sense of obligation to her: to follow through, to live up to what she expected, to fulfil his part of the bargain that they were even now kissing on each other.

He moved his hand up from her waist, up the side of her unfamiliar body and slowly, gently, his mouth still on hers, he brought his hand across to her breast. He felt her suck in her breath sharply under him, felt a reflex tension and felt her check it; then she threw her arms around him more tightly than before, giving him licence.

He stroked her bosom, then his hand went up to her neck and caressed it as an excuse to come down from there to the first buttons. He had undone two of them when she put her hand over his, pressing it to her breast, and took her mouth away.

She looked up at him with the same vaguely puzzled look, then she lifted his exploring hand and kissed it with lips which, even on his fingers, were moist and thrilling. Still clasping his hand hotly and saying nothing, she got up and led him into the bedroom . . .

4
The Good Old Days . . . and Before

As long as men have been raping and pillaging in the reputed style of the Viking raiders (*see* Chapter 1), other men have been reporting it, suitably embellished in the usual manner of newshounds, in song and legend. Unfortunately, the people who were best at raping and pillaging – the most experienced – were usually an illiterate bunch, and even if they could record their activities for posterity they usually got themselves invaded by some superior race who would change the language in the cause of progress – so precious little was ever handed down. And there was a shortage of researchers to go round chatting up the old folk, recording the songs their grandfathers used to sing, because that *wasn't* then considered progress.

Luckily, most of our western culture is inherited from the Greeks and Romans, and they were enthusiastically into sex – as you will know if you've seen the television adaptation of Robert Graves's *I Claudius*. I have to resist the temptation of starting with the Greeks, because the first recorded love song (on parchment, not tape) goes back much further, some 4000 years in all, to Sumeria (Asia Minor). Not a song in the 'pop' sense of the word, it was sung in an annual ceremony when the king took as wife a priestess of Inanna, goddess of love and procreation. Suitably overwhelmed by the honour, she would sing:

> You have captivated me, let me stand trembling before you,
> Bridegroom, I would be taken by you to the bedchamber,
> You have captivated me, let me stand trembling before you,
> Lion, I would be taken by you to the bedchamber.

I'll leave it there in deference to women readers who might not appreciate such humility from the days when a woman, even the priestess, knew her place.

The Bible is not without its share of references to sex of the illicit sort, often explicit but seldom a turn-on, although the *Song of Solomon* goes some of the way with lines like these:

> How beautiful are thy feet with shoes, O prince's daughter!
> The joints of thy thighs are like jewels, the work of the hands
> of a cunning workman.
> Thy navel is like a round goblet, which wanteth not liquor;
> Thy belly is like a heap of wheat set about with lilies.
> Thy breasts are like two young roes that are twins . . .
> How fair and how pleasant are thou, O love, for delights!

Solomon, King of Israel (970–931 BC) and son of David, is remembered for three things: wisdom, his many wives, and the beauty of the temples he erected (the desire to project the right image is surely an illustration of that wisdom). It is interesting, therefore, to reflect that the poem has sometimes been interpreted as describing the beauty not of the second speciality, but of the third, although who has ever seen a synagogue with breasts like twin roes?

We owe much to the Greeks, not least in literature and drama. The symbol of crossed masks, depicting humour and tragedy, is perhaps best represented by two remarkable writers, Sophocles (496–405 BC), and Aristophanes (*c.*444–*c.*380 BC). Sophocles, although remembered principally for tragedies such as *Antigone*, *Electra* and *Oedipus Rex*, which has been banned several times over, was an amiable fellow, skilled in music and dancing. Being particularly handsome to boot, he was chosen to lead the chorus (in the nude and carrying a strategically placed lyre) which danced about the Athenian trophy erected in 480 BC after the Battle of Salamis. I have a special affection for Aristophanes, if only for *Lysistrata* (411 BC) – one of the most brilliantly funny yet underlyingly serious plays ever written – although fifty-four comedies, of which only eleven have survived, are attributed to him.

The Athenians, you'll remember, were a cultured lot, while the Spartans were interested in little else than health and fitness, which they maintained with healthy outdoor sports, like fighting and killing. However, they were good at what they liked doing, and so the war between them and the Athenians had persisted for twenty-one years. Yet Aristophanes' approach in *Lysistrata* was not to ridicule the enemy but war itself. The play is remarkable on several levels: it is very funny, it is politically wise and it credits women with more intelligence than men. Ever since, women in the theatre have never stopped moaning 'they don't write plays for women these days'. The story is concerned basically with the disillusionment of the women of Athens. Lysistrata tells them they can end the war by refusing to have sex with their husbands until they promise to stop the fighting. A Spartan visitor agrees to persuade womenfolk on their side to do the same, and it isn't long before the men start to have second thoughts. One of the wives, Myrrhine, tantalises her husband Kinesias in a scene worthy of a Brian Rix farce; she uses every excuse under the sun not to get into bed with him until

Myrrhine: (as she comes back with a pillow) Get up.
Kinesias: But I am up.
Myrrhine: You are and all!

In due course the Spartans send envoys to discuss the situation, and Lysistrata instructs her women to escort the sexually frustrated warriors forward: 'If they refuse to give you their hands, bring them whichever way you can.' Nor did she mean by their swords.

Greek culture was fostered and developed by Rome, until the slide into decadence got out of hand. And in best-seller terms, the Harold Robbins of his day was Ovid (43 BC–AD17), whose *Ars Amatoria* (Art of Love) was nothing much more than a pleasantly presented tract on sexual relations in three parts; the first part offers advice to men on how to obtain a mistress and the second on how to keep her, while the third instructed women on how to satisfy men.

Ovid was a successful lawyer until an inheritance from his father's estate enabled him to concentrate on poetry and – good living. In AD 9 he was banished by the Emperor Augustus, ostensibly because of his poetry. This was in character, since Augustus, unlike his successors, had high moral standards. But Ovid's writing, while mildly erotic, was never shocking, and a more likely reason was that, because of the debauched company he kept, he knew something about the Emperor's beloved but nymphomaniac granddaughter Julia that was dangerous to her reputation. Ovid died in exile.

An appreciation and enjoyment of foreign languages depends much on the translators. Emile Zola, for example, has been done a disservice by many translators who could not fail to recapture the tremendous power of his narrative, but missed the excitement and colour of less sombre passages. Some of Zola's prose about sexual relations is highly erotic, yet frequently translated into flat, uninspired, almost mechanical prose. A translator needs to get into the *spirit* of the author's words. There have been many competent English versions of Ovid's *Art of Love*, but in 1957 Rolfe Humphries produced a modern version one feels Ovid might have enjoyed. The following extracts make my point:

They do not need to be teased, to be worked up into a frenzy,
They can keep up with a man – yes, and a good thing, too.
What I like is the deal that leaves both partners exhausted;
That's why I find no joy in the embrace of a boy.
Duty is all very well, but let's not confuse it with pleasure;
I do not want any girl doing her duty for me.
What I like to hear are the words of utter abandon,
Words that say, 'Not too soon!' words that say, 'Wait just a
while.'
Let me see my girl with eyes that confess her excitement;
Let her, after she comes, want no more for a while.
What does youth know of delight? Some things ought not to
be hurried.
After some thirty-odd years, lovers begin to learn how!

From Book II (satisfying a mistress)

Lie on your back, if your face and all of your features are pretty
If your posterior's cute, better be seen from behind.
Milanion used to bear Atalanta's legs on his shoulders;
If you have beautiful legs, let them be lifted like hers.
Little girls do all right if they sit on top, riding horseback;
Hector's Andromache knew she could not do this; too tall!
Press the couch with your knees and bend your back
backwards a little,
If your view, full-length, seems what a love should crave,
If the breasts and thighs are lovely to look at,
Let the man stand and the girl lie on a slant on the bed.

From Book III (satisfying a man)

Historians differ when judging the Emperor Tiberius (42 BC–AD

37), step-son of Augustus, but according to Suetonius in *The Twelve Caesars* (translated by Robert Graves):

> On retiring to Capri he made himself a private sporting-house, where sexual extravagances were practised for his secret pleasure. Bevies of girls and young men, whom he had collected from all over the Empire as adepts in unnatural practices, and known as *spintriae*, would perform before him in groups of three, to excite his waning passions. A number of small rooms were furnished with the most indecent pictures and statuary obtainable, also certain erotic manuals from Elephantis in Egypt; the inmates of the establishment would know from these exactly what was expected of them.

The poetess Elephantis, one of several women writers on pornographic themes, is supposed to have dwelt at some length on the different sexual positions in coitus.

Only a few years after the death of Tiberius, the author whose name was on everyone's lips was Caius Petronius, whose greatest work was *The Satyricon*, first published in England by the Edward Curll mentioned earlier. The few remaining fragments of his other works to survive include *Trimalchio's Feast* and *The Matron of Ephesus*, the story of a beautiful and virtuous widow, copied a hundred years later by Apuleius in his *Golden Ass*. Some of the writing of Petronius contained contemporary Latin slang of the sort associated with lavatory walls and, in fact, it probably inspired much of the graffiti found at Pompeii. Petronius committed suicide at the 'suggestion' of Nero, on what was almost certainly a trumped-up charge of treason.

The *Satires* of Juvenal (*c*AD 60–140) have been compared with Swift. Like Swift, Juvenal not only had strong views on political issues, but knew a lot about human nature. Only sixteen of the *Satires* still exist and that *On Women* (part vi) has a passage about a Roman wife who would flog her servants as a means of stimulation before meeting her lover, or even watch them being beaten if she was feeling frustrated at her husband's lack of interest in bed the previous night:

> Tis worth a little labour, to survey
> Our wives more near, and trace 'em through the day.
> If, dreadful to relate! the night foregone,
> The husband turn'd his back, or lay alone,

All, all is lost; the housekeeper is stripp'd,
The tiremaid chidden, and the chairman whipp'd:
Rods, cords, and thongs, avenge the master's sleep,
Add force the guiltless house to wake, and weep.

There are, who hire a beadle by the year,
To last their servants round; who, pleased to hear
The eternal thong, bid him lay on, while they,
At perfect ease, the milkman's stores survey,
Chat with their female gossips, or replace
The crack'd enamel on their treacherous face,
No respite yet: – they leisurely him o'er
The countless *items* of the day before,
And bid him still lay on; till, faint with toil,

He drops the scourge; when with a rancorous smile,
'Begone!' they thunder in a horrid tone,
'Now your accounts are settled, rogues begone!'

But should she wish with nicer care to dress,
And now the hour of assignation press,
(Whether the adulterer, for her coming, wait
In Isis' fane, to bawdry consecrate.
Or in Lucullus' walks) the house appears,
A true Sicilian court, all gloom and tears.
The wretched Psecas, for the whip prepared,
With locks dishevell'd, and with shoulders bared,
Attempts her hair; fire flashes from her eyes,
And, 'Strumpet! why this curl so high?' she cries.
Instant the lash, without remorse, is plied,
And the blood stains her bosom, back, and side.

(This translation at the end of the eighteenth century is by William Gifford (1756–1826) first editor of the *Quarterly Review*.)

Lucius Apuleius (born *c.* AD 125) made his points about human frailties by substituting farce for cynicism in his satirical *Metamorphoses* or *The Golden Ass*, which has been described as a 'parent' of modern romantic literature. Born in North Africa, he was educated at Carthage and Athens and, after inheriting a small fortune from his father, travelled extensively in Italy and Asia. His experiences formed the framework for the book, a series of bizarre adventures in which the hero (Apuleius) is at one stage turned into a donkey. The following excerpt concerns his wooing of the servant girl, Fotis. Again, there are several versions in English, but it is interesting to reflect on how our Elizabethan ancestors would have reacted to the translation of William Adlington in 1566:

> Then I unable to sustaine the broiling heate that I was in, ran upon her and kissed the place where she had thus laid her haire. Whereat she turned her face, and cast her rolling eyes upon me, saying, O Scholler, thou hast tasted now both hony and gall, take heed that thy pleasure do not turne into repentance. Tush (quoth I) my sweet heart, I am contented for such another kisse to be broiled here upon this fire, wherwithall I embraced and kissed her more often, and shee embraced and kissed me likewise, and moreover her breath smelled like Cinnamon, and the liquor of her tongue was like unto sweet Nectar, wherewith when my mind was greatly delighted I sayd, Behold Fotis I am yours, and shall presently dye unlesse you take pity upon me. Which when I had said she eftsoone kissed me, and bid me be of good courage, and I will (quoth shee) satisfie your whole desire, and it shall be no longer delayed than until night, when as assure your selfe I will come and lie with you: wherfore go your wayes and prepare your selfe, for I intend valiantly and couragiously to encounter with you this night. Thus when we had lovingly talked and reasoned together, we departed for that time. . . .
>
> Thus when I had well replenished my self with wine, and was now ready unto Venery not onely in minde but also in body, I removed my cloathes, and shewing to Fotis my great impatiencie I sayd, O my sweet heart take pitty upon me and helpe me, for as you see I am now prepared unto the battell, which you your selfe did appoint: for after that I felt the first Arrow of cruell Cupid within my breast, I bent my bow very strong, and now feare (because it is bended so hard) lest my string should breake: but that thou mayst the better please me, undresse they haire and come and embrace mee lovingly; whereupon she made no long delay, but set aside all the meat and wine, and then she unapparelled her selfe, and unattyred her haire, presenting her amiable body unto me in manner of faire Venus, when shee goeth under the waves of the sea. Now (quoth shee) is come the houre of justing, now is come the

time of warre, wherefore shew thy selfe like unto a man, for I will not retyre, I will not fly the field, see then thou bee valiant, see thou be couragious, since there is no time appointed when our skirmish shall cease. In saying these words she came to me to bed, and embraced me sweetly, and so wee passed all the night in pastime and pleasure, and never slept until it was day: but wee would eftsoones refresh our wearinesse, and provoke our pleasure, and renew our venery by drinking of wine. In which sort we pleasantly passed away many other nights following.

The Britons weren't the most cultured of folk, even after a few centuries of Roman occupation. They weren't exactly thick, but let us say they didn't know how to express themselves. The Anglo-Saxons weren't that much better, but at least their monks could read and write, and collectively they were responsible for compiling the *Exeter Book* (*Codex Exoniensis*), an anthology of Old English tales and religious poems. The collection remains one of the most important sources of Old English verse but also lays claim to being Britain's first 'pornographic' book since many of some eighty riddles have double meanings. The original manuscript was presented to Exeter Cathedral by Leofric, Bishop of Exeter between 1050 and 1071. Here are just three of the riddles to which, curiously, no answers were given. You, of course, with pure minds will not need to be told the answers, but for the sake of your less worthy friends I have listed them at the end:

Riddle No 44

Splendidly it hangs by a man's thigh, under the master's cloak. In front is a hole. It is stiff and hard; it has a goodly place. When the man lifts his own garment up above the knee, he wishes to visit with the head of this hanging instrument the familiar hole he had often filled with equal length.

No 54

There came a young man where he knew her to be standing in a corner. The lusty batchelor went up to her from a distance, lifted up his own garment with his hands, and thrust something stiff under her girdle where she stood, wrought his will; both of them shook. The thane hurried; his good servant was sometimes useful; nevertheless though strong, he always became tired, and weary of the work, sooner than she. There began to grow under her girdle what good men often love in their hearts and buy with money.

No 62

I am hard and sharp, resolute in my going forth, active in my journey onwards, faithful to my lord. I go under a belly and I clear for myself a straight path. The man is in haste, the hero who pushes me from behind with the help of his dress. Sometimes he draws me out hot from the hole, sometimes again takes me somewhere into a narrow place; the man from the south presses me vigorously. Say what I am called.

(The answers, in order, are a key, a milk churn and a poker.)

The Renaissance, a milestone in literature as well as the other arts, saw four books that were to become classics published within a hundred years or so. All had the same format, a collection of tales related by one or several people, but all came from different countries, although at least a couple were inspired by another. The first, and therefore most original, was *The Decameron* by Giovanni Boccaccio (1313–75) who conceived the idea of seven girls and three young men of good families 'marooned' in a luxury villa just outside Florence during a plague in the city. Each tells one story a day for ten days, hence the title. Published in Venice in 1371, the book was to become one of the first to be copied when printing was invented and therefore reached a wider audience than had been thought possible only a few years before.

Several of the stories had an erotic element, yet when the book was eventually banned by the Church it was not for this reason, but for the irreverent treatment of the men of God who featured in the stories. Typical of them is 'How to Put the Devil in Hell', told on the third day about a Tunisian girl, Alibech, who is advised that the best way to serve God as a Christian is to renounce the world. She goes off into the desert and there meets a hermit, Rustico, who volunteers to instruct her in the ways of the Lord. Although he is a young man, she treats him with the respect due to a holy man, and so when he strips to pray, the girl copies him, falling naked to her knees:

Matters standing thus and Rustico being more than ever inflamed in his desires to see her so fair, there came the resurrection of the flesh, which Alibech observing and marvelling, 'Rustico,' quoth she, 'what is that I see on thee which thrusts forth thus and which I have not?' 'Faith, daughter mine,' answered he, 'this is the Devil whereof I bespoke thee; and see now, he giveth me such sore annoy that I can scarce put up with it.' Then said the girl, 'Now praised be God! I see I fare better than thou, in that I have none of yonder Devil.' 'True,' rejoined Rustico, 'but thou hast other what that I have not, and thou hast it instead of this.' 'What is that?' asked Alibech; and he, 'Thou hast hell, and I tell thee methinketh God hath sent thee thither for my soul's health, for that, whereas this devil doth me this awry, and it please thee have so much compassion on me as to suffer me to put him back into hell, thou wilt give me the utmost solacement and wilt do God a very great pleasure and service, so indeed thou be come into these parts to do as thou sayst.'

The girl answered in good faith, 'Marry, father mine, since I have hell, be it whensoever it pleaseth thee,' whereupon quoth Rustico, 'Daughter, blessed be thou; let us go then and put him back there, so he may after leave me in peace.' So saying, he laid her on one of their little beds and taught her how she should do to imprison that accursed one of God. The girl, who had never put any devil in hell, for the first time felt some little pain; wherefore she said to Rustico, 'Certes, father mine, this same devil must be an ill thing and an enemy in very deed of God, for that it irketh hell itself let it be otherwhat when he is put back therein.' 'Daughter,' answered Rustico, 'it will not always happen thus,' and to the end this should not happen, six times, or ever they stirred from the bed, they put him in hell again, insomuch that for the nonce they so took the conceit out of his head that he willingly abode in peace. But it returning to him again and again the ensuing days and the obedient girl still lending herself to take it out of him, it befell that the sport began to please her and she said to Rustico, 'I see now that those good people in Tunis spoke sooth, when they avouched that it was so sweet a thing to serve God; for certes, I remember me not to have ever done aught that afforded me such pleasance and delight as putting the devil in hell; wherefore methinketh that who so applieth himself unto aught other than God His service is a fool.'

Accordingly, she came oft-times to Rustico and said to him, 'Father mine, I came here to serve God and not to abide idle; let us put the devil in hell.' Which doing, she said whiles, 'Rustico, I know not why the devil fleeth away from hell; for if he abode there as willingly as hell receiveth him and holdeth him, he would never come forth therefrom.' The girl, so preoccupied with this problem began to exhort Rustico to the service of God, which so took the bombast out of doublet that he felt cold what time another had sweated; wherefore he fell to telling her that the devil was not to be chastised nor put in hell, save when as he should lift up his head for pride; 'and we,' added he, 'by God's grace have so baffled him that he prayeth our Lord to suffer him abide in peace,' and on this tack he for a time imposed silence on her. However, when she said that he required her not of putting the devil in hell, she said to him one day, 'Rustico, if thy devil be chastened and give thee no more annoy, my hell letteth me not be, wherefore thou wilt do well to aid me with thy devil abating the raging of my hell, even as with my hell I have helped thee take the conceit out of thy devil.'

Rustico, who lived on roots and water, could ill avail to answer her calls and told her that it would need over-many devils to appease hell, but he would do what he might thereof. Accordingly he satisfied her bytimes, but so seldom it was but casting a bean into the lion's mouth; whereat the girl, her seeming she served not God as diligently, as she would fain have done, murmured somewhat.

(translation by John Payne, 1886)

Chaucer, whose middle-English language has undoubtedly protected him from the wrath of the moralists, went to Florence as a young man, and subsequently (1391–9) wrote *The Canterbury Tales*, in which the stories are told by thirty pilgrims. On the strength of the *Tales*, Chaucer is ranked alongside Shakespeare as one of the greatest of English writers. Unfortunately he died in 1400 before completing them. He is read these days mainly by students who, despite 'translations' and various teaching aids, seldom realise what he was alluding to; if they do, they have usually already read books a lot bawdier.

Several of Chaucer's stories have a high proportion of 'bad' language as well as eroticism, although they are so full of joy and life that it is hard to imagine anyone taking offence. As an example, read the story of the elderly carpenter's young wife in *The Miller's Tale*, who is serenaded by Absalom; he won't leave without a kiss. She unbars the window and:

Dark was the night as pitch, aye dark as coal,
And through the window she put out her hole,
And Absalom no better felt nor worse,
But with his mouth he kissed her naked arse.

The wife in the *Wife of Bath* asks one of her husbands:

What ails you that grumble so and groan?
Is it because you'd have my cunt alone?

The Wife of Bath incidentally has had five husbands and gives an account of her sex life, making it clear who her favourite was:

And now of my fifth husband will I tell,
God grant his soul may never get to Hell!
And yet he was to me most brutal, too;
My ribs yet feel as they were black and blue,
And ever shall until my dying day.
But in our bed he was so fresh and gay,
And therewithal he could so well impose,
What time he wanted use of my *belle chose*,
That though he's beaten me in every bone,
He could re-win my love, and that full soon.
I guess I loved him best of all, for he
Gave of his love most sparingly to me.

L'Heptameron or *Histoires des Amans Fortunez*, inspired by *The Decameron*, has its storytellers trapped by a flood and recounting their tales over ten days, although the author, Marguerite d'Angoulême (1492–1547), Queen of Navarre, died when she had completed only seven of the sections. Not only was Margaret one of the most beautiful women of the age, but a humane person by the standards of the time (protecting Protestants from persecution), highly intelligent and a patron of the arts. One of the talented writers who benefited from her patronage was Françoïs Rabelais (1490–1553), a monk turned physician, who gave his name to a racy and colourful style of 'clean' but bawdy humour. Margaret had published poetry and works of a more serious nature, and these sexy tales were produced eleven years after her death, under their subtitle – being reprinted in 1559 with the title which has become so famous.

The fourth of the Renaissance classics was, of course, *The Arabian*

Nights' Entertainments, or *The Thousand and One Nights*, which are supposed to have originated in India around 1500 and come to the attention of western scholars via Persia. The stories were introduced to Europe 200 years later by a Frenchman who copied them down as they were told to him. Discovering that his bride had been unfaithful, the Sultan decreed that future wives should be executed on the morning after the marriage. But when he marries Scheherazade she embarks on a series of stories so enthralling that by breaking off every night in the middle the execution has to be postponed so that he can hear the end of the story. The process was repeated for 1001 nights until the Sultan realised his original decree had become a bit pointless.

Many of the stories are wide-eyed accounts of impressively powerful couplings.

> He went into the room where my lady was and passed all the night with her in charges, assaults, and other games. I was able to hear all they did and to count on my fingers the number of nails they drove, because of the astonishing noise which they made in doing it. 'As Allah lives,' I thought, 'they must have built a blacksmith's forge on the bed! The iron bar must be very hot to make the anvil groan so much!'

I may have bent the rules slightly by including *L'Heptameron* among the group of four classics, because it fitted the pattern more directly, before discussing what was probably the first French classic, *Les Cent Nouvelles Nouvelles* (*One Hundred Stories*), the authorship of which was also attributed to royalty, this time Louis XI. This was probably a bit of fifteenth-century salesmanship: certainly the book did well. Within a century it had arrived in England where it was given the marvellous title *One Hundred Merrie and Delightsome Stories: Right Pleasant to Relate in All Goodly Companie by Way of Joyance and Jollity*. It understandably became popular in England, but did not have the lasting quality of the others mentioned. However, one of the stories, *The Reverse of the Medal*, stands the test of time (the nineteenth-century translator is unknown):

> In the town of Valenciennes there lived formerly a notable citizen, who had been receiver of Hainault, who was renowned amongst all others for his prudence and discretion, and amongst his praiseworthy virtues, liberality was not the least, and thus it came

to pass that he enjoyed the grace of princes, lords, and other persons of good estate. And this happy condition, Fortune granted and preserved him to the end of his days.

Both before and after death unloosed him from the chains of matrimony, the good citizen mentioned in this story, was not so badly lodged in the said town but that many a great lord would have been content and honoured to have such a lodging. His house faced several streets, in one of which was a little postern door, opposite to which lived a good comrade of his, who had a pretty wife, still young and charming.

And as is customary, her eyes, the archers of the heart, shot so many arrows into the said citizen, that unless he found some present remedy, he felt his case was no less than mortal.

To more surely prevent such a fate, he found many and subtle manners of making the good comrade, the husband of the said queen, his private and familiar friend, so that few of the dinners, suppers, banquets, baths, and other amusements took place, either in the hotel or elsewhere, without his company. And of such favours his comrade was very proud, and also happy.

When our citizen, who was more cunning than a fox, had gained the good-will of his friend, little was needed to win the love of his wife, and in a few days he had worked so much and so well that the gallant lady was fain to hear his case, and to provide a suitable remedy thereto. It remained but to provide time and place; and for this she promised him that, whenever her husband lay abroad for a night, she would advise him thereof.

The wished-for day arrived when the husband told his wife that he was going to a chateau some three leagues distant from Valenciennes, and charged her to look after the house and keep within doors, because his business would not permit him to return that night.

It need not be asked if she was joyful, though she showed it not either in word, or deed, or otherwise. Her husband had not journeyed a league before the citizen knew that the opportunity had come.

He caused the baths to be brought forth, and the stoves to be heated, and pasties, tarts, and hippocras, and all the rest of God's good gifts, to be prepared largely and magnificently.

When evening came, the postern door was unlocked, and she who was expected entered thereby, and she was kindly received.

Then they ascended into a chamber, and washed in a bath, by

the side of which a good supper was quickly laid and served. They drank often and deeply. *To speak of the wines and viands would be a waste of time and, to cut the story short, there was plenty of everything.* (My italics – RHL). In this most happy condition passed the great part of this sweet but short night; kisses often given and often returned, until they desired nothing but to go to bed.

Whilst they were thus making good cheer, the husband returned from his journey, and knowing nothing of this adventure, knocked loudly at the door of the house. And the company that was in the ante-chamber refused him entrance until he should name his surety.

Then he gave his name loud and clear, and so his good wife and the citizen heard him and knew him. She was so amazed to hear the voice of her husband that her loyal heart almost failed her; and she would have fainted, had not the good citizen and his servants comforted her.

The good citizen being calm and well advised how to act, made haste to put her to bed, and lay close by her; and charged her well that she should lie close to him and hide her face, so that no one could see it. And that being done as quickly as may be, yet without too much haste, he ordered that the door should be opened. Then his good comrade sprang into the room, thinking to himself that there must be some mystery, else they had not kept him out of the room. And when he saw the table laid with wines and goodly viands, also the bath finely prepared, and the citizen in a handsome bed, well curtained, with a second person by his side, he spoke loudly, and praised the good cheer of his neighbour. He called him rascal, and whoremonger, and drunkard, and many other names, which made those who were in the chamber laugh long and loud; but his wife could not join in the mirth, her face being pressed to the side of her new friend.

'Ha!' said the husband. 'Master whoremonger, you have well hidden from me this good cheer; but, by my faith, though I was not at the feast, you must show me the bride.'

And with that, holding a candle in his hand, he drew near the bed, and would have withdrawn the coverlet, under which, in fear and silence, lay his most good and perfect wife; when the citizen and his servants prevented him; but he was not content, and would by force, in spite of them all, have laid his hand upon the bed.

But he was not master there, and could not have his will, and for good cause, and was fain to be content with a most gracious proposal which was made to him, and which was this, that he should be shown the back-side of his wife, and her haunches, and thighs – which were big and white, and moreover fair and comely – without uncovering and beholding her face.

The good comrade, still holding a candle in his hand, gazed for long without saying a word; and when he did speak, it was to praise highly the great beauty of that dame, and he swore by a great oath that he had never seen anything that so much resembled the back parts of his own wife, and that were he not well sure that she was at home at that time, he would have said it was she.

She had by this somewhat recovered, and he drew back much disconcerted, but they all told him, first one and then the other, that he had judged wrongly, and spoken against the honour of his wife, and that this was some other woman, as he would afterwards see for himself.

To restore him to good humour, after they had thus paused his eyes, the citizen ordered that they should make him sit at the table, where he drowned his suspicions by eating and drinking of what was left of the supper, whilst they in the bed were robbing him of his honour.

The time came to leave, and he said goodnight to the citizen and his companions, and begged they would let him leave by the postern door, that he might the sooner return home. But the citizen replied that he knew not where to find the key; he thought also that the lock was so rusted that they could not open the door, which they rarely if ever used. He was content therefore to leave by the front gate, and make a long detour to reach his house, and whilst the servants of the citizen led him to the door, the good wife was quickly on her feet, and in a short time, clad in a simple sark with her corset on her arm, and come to the postern. She made but one bound to her house, where she awaited her husband (who came by a longer way) well prepared as to the manner in which she should receive him.

Soon came our man, and seeing still a light in the house, knocked at the door loudly; and this good wife, who was pretending to clean the house, and had a besom in her hands, asked – what she knew well; 'Who is there?'

And he replied; 'It is your husband.'

'My husband!' said she. 'My husband is not here! He is not in the town!'

With that he knocked again, and cried, 'Open the door! I am your husband.'

'I know my husband well,' quoth she, 'and it is not his custom to return home so late at night, when he is in the town. Go away, and do not knock here at this hour.'

But he knocked all the more, and called her by name once or twice. Yet she pretended not to know him, and asked why he came at that hour, but for all reply he said nothing but, 'Open! Open!'

'Open!' said she. 'What! are you still there you rascally whoremonger? By St. Mary, I would rather see you drown than come in here! Go! and sleep as badly as you please in the place where you came from.'

Then her good husband grew angry, and thundered against the door as though he would knock the house down, and threatened to beat his wife, such was his rage, – of which she had not great fear; but at length, because of the noise he made, and that she might the better speak her mind to him, she opened the door, and when he entered, he saw an angry face, and had a warm greeting. For when her tongue found words from a heart overcharged with anger and indignation, her language was sharp as well-ground Guingant razors.

And, amongst other things, she reproached him that he had wickedly pretended a journey in order that he might try her, and that he was a coward and a recreant, unworthy to have such a wife as she was. . . .

The poor man, much grieved, seeing his wife more troubled than he liked, knew not what to say. And his suspicions being removed, he drew near her, weeping and falling upon his knees and made the following fine speech:

'My most dear companion, and most loyal wife, I beg and pray of you to remove from your heart the wrath you have conceived against me, and pardon me for all that I have done against you. I own my fault, I see my error. I have come now from a place where they made good cheer, and where, I am ashamed to say, I fancied I recognized you, at which I was much displeased. And so I wrongfully and causelessly suspected you to be other than a good woman, of which I now repent bitterly, and pray of you to forgive me, and pardon my folly.'

The good woman, seeing her husband so contrite, showed no great anger.

'What?' said she, 'You have come from filthy houses of ill-fame, and you dare to think that your honest wife would be seen in such places?'

'No, no, my dear, I know you would not. I beseech you, say no more about it,' said the good man, and repeated his aforesaid request.

She, seeing his contrition, ceased her reproaches, and little by little regained her composure, and with much ado pardoned him, after he had made a hundred thousand oaths and promises to her who had so wronged him. And from that time forth she often, without fear or regret, passed the said postern, nor were her escapades discovered by him who was most concerned.

One of the first names that springs to mind when collecting antiquarian erotica or pornography is Pietro Aretino (1492–1556), although the degree to which his works are sought depends much on the illustrations supplied in each edition. Aretino was not the sort of man one could ignore; he was a loudmouth one either accepted or disliked. His outspokenness earned him the title 'The Scourge of Princes', although since his views were generally extreme, his criticisms were usually of the poison-pen variety. Nor did he hesitate to try his hand at blackmail when money was a little short, offering for a small consideration a little 'plug' in the scandal sheet he edited, or even demanding money for *not* publishing something unsavoury. He was invariably in trouble but enjoyed the patronage of men of power such as Giulio de Medici and François I of France.

One of the scandals which caused him to leave Rome for a while erupted over his writing of the lascivious sonnets, *Sonetti Lussuriosi*, which he claims were done as a commentary for and (inspired by) sixteen drawings of different sexual positions by his artist friend, Giulio Romano, who had them engraved by Marcantonio Raimondi.

Although principally a poet and playright, he also published some 3000 letters, which threw considerable light on sixteenth-century life and which caused latterday admirers to refer to him as the first modern journalist. In one of these letters (to Battista Zatti) he claimed to have dedicated his sonnets to 'the hypocrites, out of patience with their villainous judgement and with the hoggish custom that forbids the eyes what delights them'. In a biographical foreword to the *Works of Aretino* (privately printed for Rarity Press Inc, New York, 1931), by an unnamed author, he is described as 'the first writer who dared break away from the old, dead and deadening, hide-bound traditions of the classicists and the academicians and to write in the language of the people, the language of the street and the market place, even that of the brothel'.

Much of Aretino's eroticism depends on the skill of the illustrator since, while the author sets a scene admirably, he is usually content to leave something to the imagination. In the *Ragionamenti* (his *Dialogues*), for example, he portrays the life of three classes of woman – nun, wife and courtesan – reaching the conclusion that the life of the courtesan is the best and most honourable. The following brief extract from 'The Life of Married Women' shows Aretino's interest in love-making. The wife is seventeen years old and beautiful; her husband old, a bore and impotent. Frustrated, she gets a limited kick out of riding him like a horse, but this is not enough, and she devises a plan:

> **Nanna:** [telling the story] She began talking in her sleep at night, speaking in disconnected words, which at first caused the old dotard to cackle loudly, but when she came to double up her little fist and give him a swat in the eye, so that he had to poultice it with oil of rose-water, he reproved her for it greatly. But she pretended not to remember what she had done or said, and in addition, she began leaving her bed, opening windows and trunks, and sometimes, she even went so far as to dress herself, whereupon the old fool would run after her, shaking all over and calling after her in a loud voice; and on one occasion it happened that, in his efforts to follow her out the door of a room, setting foot to the top of a stair which he thought led to the ground, he fell all the way down and broke himself all over, fracturing a leg and raising such an uproar that the family, on hearing his cries, which had aroused the neighbourhood, came running to him and picked him up – though it would have served him right, if he had never got up. And she, pretending she had been awakened by her husband's cries, on hearing what had happened, fell to weeping and grieved greatly, cursing the vice of sleep-walking; and night as it was, she straightway sent for the doctor to put the bones back in place.
>
> **Antonia:** What was her object in pretending to be dreaming?
>
> **Nanna:** Just to get him to fall, so that, breaking his bones, he wouldn't be able to follow her. And at this, the big baby, in his jealousy, was more miserable than ever, but so vain, with his broken heart, that he had ten big strapping grooms lodged in a large hall on the ground floor. The oldest of them was not more

than twenty-four, and a misfit lot they were: the one that had a good cap had socks full of holes, and the one that had good socks had a worse doublet, and the one with a good doublet had a disastrous cloak, and the one with a good cloak had a ragged shirt; and they lived on bread and capers.

Antonia: Why did the rogues put up with it?

Nanna: Because of the liberty he gave them. And now, Antonia dear, this lady of ours had given a look at this company; and since she had the old blockhead safe in bed, with his thighs between a pair of splints, she resumed her dreaming, and, throwing her arms about and crying always 'O la! O la!,' she would jump out of bed and, opening the door, she would leave him to strangle with calling for her. And then, she would go to the grooms who, around a lamp that was always about to sputter out, were gambling away a few farthings which they had stolen from their master in the purchase of trifles. Giving them goodnight, she would put out the light, and drawing upon her the first that came to hand, she would commence to sport with him, and in three hours which she spent with them, she would try them all ten, twice for each one; and returning up above, freed of the humours which had caused her to go rambling about, she would say: 'My husband, it is this cursed nature of mine which, like a witch, forces me to go prowling about the house all night.'

As you might have noticed from the examples I've given, writers of the late Middle Ages and early Renaissance seemed to have been inspired by cuckoldry, and the superior wit and intellect of wives and mistresses – idiot husbands were obviously their equivalent of the twentieth century's Irishman.

The son of a lady-in-waiting to Queen Margaret of Navarre was Pierre Bourdeille (*c.* 1540–1614), who became better known as the Seigneur de Brantôme, author of the *Lives of the Fair and Gallant Ladies*. First published in nine volumes, 1665–6, this has been produced repeatedly in sumptuously bound private and limited editions, usually in only two volumes, although most of the erotic passages are not translated.

Brantôme is another who played on the thick husband tradition. In Volume I's *First Discourse: of ladies Which Do Not Make Love, and Their Husbands' Cuckolds*, allegedly writing from experience, he talks at length about chastity and ways of overcoming the problem, for example the wife who would permit lovers to do whatever they wished except kiss her on the mouth, since this was the only part of her anatomy she had promised specifically to save for her husband; and another who would agree to intercourse only in the dominant position so she could still swear on oath that no man had mounted her.

In dealing with lesbianism, Brantôme is just as frank, but most of his translators have ducked the challenge. A. R. Allinson, considered one of the best translators, would leave certain spicy passages in French, but in places keep even French readers in suspense, as for example in Brantôme's description of the profitable use of dildoes: *Cette façon n'apporte point de dommage, ce disent aucuns, comme quand on s'aide d'instruments façonnés de . . . . mais qu'on voulu appeler des g—.* (NB: *g*=godemiche=dildo.)

He goes on to describe how a couple of young women are caught in the act of using this natural-looking dildo.

> One of them was surprised in the act and found to be fitted with a great one between her legs, fastened so prettily with little straps around her body that it seemed like a natural member. She was caught so suddenly that the Prince did actually constrain her to show him how the pair of them did the thing betwixt them.

However, while leaving little to the imagination, Brantôme was hardly an erotic writer; more a peeping tom with a sense of humour.

That William Shakespeare (1564–1616) was a genius there can be little doubt; and one of the most fascinating aspects of his work is the remarkable understanding of human nature it displays. Shakespeare had even less education than some of his contemporaries; he presumably learnt from observation and his own experience (and he managed to live a full life), but when he started writing there wasn't much to draw on. He was little more than a provincial lad finding his feet in the big city. Many passages among his prolific writings are erotic in various degrees, but since in the west we tend to be preoccupied with his plays, let's look at an early poem, 'Venus and Adonis (1593)'. If you can accept the supposition that a healthy young man (who is not gay) would be able to resist passionate advances from the Sophia Loren of his day, then Shakespeare certainly knew how to capture the taut, uneasy atmosphere of unrequited lust. Venus, on heat, has plucked Adonis from his horse and is doing her best to seduce him. Eventually he offers her one kiss if she'll let him go:

Now quick desire hath caught the yielding prey,
And glutton-like she feeds, yet never filleth;
Her lips are conquerors, his lips obey,
Paying what ransom the insulter willeth;
  Whose vulture thought doth pitch the price so high,
  That she will draw his lips' rich treasure dry.

And having felt the sweetness of the spoil,
With blindfold fury she begins to forage;
Her face doth reek and smoke, her blood doth boil,
And careless lust stirs up a desperate courage;
  Planting oblivion, beating reason back,
  Forgetting shame's pure blush and honour's wrack.

Shakespeare's talented contemporary Christopher Marlowe (born 1564, killed in 1593 in a tavern brawl over money, although some say he was murdered, because of his political views) was a playwright of considerable stature. But as a poet he also had a romantic streak, as demonstrated by his *Come Live With Me, and Be My Love*, his translation of Ovid's *Amores* and his unfinished version of the *Hero and Leander* legend, which was published in 1598 having been completed by George Chapman, better known as a translator from Latin. In this there's a happier ending. After a preliminary skirmish, which leaves Leander unsatisfied, he swims the Hellespont to continue his siege. Hero jumps out of bed to answer his call, but jumps back under the covers when she sees him naked. Leander joins her (he needs to get warm again after his long swim) and eventually her defences start to lower:

And now she lets him whisper in her ear,
Flatter, entreet, promise, protest and swear,
Yet ever as he greedily assay'd
To touch those dainties, she the harpy play'd,
And every limb did as a soldier stout
Defend the fort, and keep the foeman out.
For though the rising ivory mount he scal'd,

Which is with azure circling lines empal'd,
Much like a globe (a globe, may I term this,
By which love sails to regions full of bliss),
Yet there with Sisyphus toil'd in vain,
Till gently parley did the truce obtain,
Wherein Leander on her quivering breast,
Breathless spoke something, and sigh'd out the rest;
Which so prevail'd, as he with small ado
Enclos'd her in his arms, and kiss'd her too;
And every kiss to her was as a charm,
And to Leander as a fresh alarm;
So that the truce was broke, and she alas,
Poor silly maiden at his mercy was.

Writers in England, and there was an abundance of talent during the 'golden' age of Elizabeth, made hay while the sun shone; little did they know it, but the stultifying Puritan revolution was only a generation away. We could not leave the sixteenth century without looking at a very famous erotic work from another part of the world, *The Golden Lotus* (*Chin P'ing Mei*) of Wang Shih-cheng (died 1593), translated by Clement Egerton in four volumes. The book derives its title from the fifth wife of the hero, Hsi-men Ching, and concerns itself with not only the couple's sexual activities but with those of their family and servants – a cast of some 150! Whether it has something to do with the westerner's natural curiosity about China and the Orient, or whether the style is so delightfully natural and uninhibited, the most apparently pornographic passages do not (or should not) cause offence, whether we're concerned with the Chinese equivalent of swinging from the chandeliers, a variety of perversions, or a predilection for sex aids. Here is just one example:

Hsi-men took off Golden Lotus' ornate scarlet-coloured slippers, loosened the ribbons which bound her feet and tied them to the trellis so that she seemed like a golden dragon showing its claws. The woman's portal was wide open, and her purple valley was clearly visible and exposed to the vigilant watchman. . . .

Hsi-men took from a pocket in his gown a case of love instruments. First he put on the clasp, and tied a sulphur ring about the root of evil. Not wishing to lance her, he played for a long while around the opening so that the woman cried furiously: 'My sweetheart, my darling, either be a man quickly or I'll go out of my mind.'

With one blow he seemed to penetrate her to the very marrow. Then he withdrew, and searched his pockets until he found the powder which procures a woman's pleasure. Smearing his weapon therewith, he thrust it into the frog's mouth. He attacked again, and instantly the warrior appeared tall and proud, full of fiery ardour. While Hsi-men admired his assault, Golden Lotus, lying on the mat, murmured with half closed eyes: 'O my bearded delight! O most magnificent of members! My darling, you don't know what you're putting into me. Your thing arouses me to fury. Spare me, I pray.' Thus she pleaded shamelessly; but Hsi-men, putting his hands upon the mat to brace himself, straightway attacked with all his strength, now pulling out and anon stabbing in, charging down a hundred times to the deepest point before again withdrawing. The woman wiped off her tender blossom with a napkin, but to no avail. Her spring continued to trickle; and the warrior, still hard and ferocious, did not wish to stop fighting. 'It is time,' exclaimed Hsi-men, 'for the monk to strike the gong.' With a sudden thrust he reached the inmost arch, where within the gateway of the feminine citadel there lies what is life unto the stamen of a flower which, when touched by the victor, is affected with a wonderful pleasure. Golden Lotus felt pain and drew herself back, but inside her body the sulphur ring had already rattled and broken.

She closed her eyes and her breath came faintly; only a faint murmur issued from her lips, the top of her tongue became icy cold, and her body fell back lifeless upon the mat.

Anal intercourse is a favourite pastime with various women in the book.

Soon she murmured again: 'My life, my joy, wouldn't you again like to pluck love's fruit at the back door?' He turned the woman over on her belly and advanced his mighty warrior. His attack was so violent as to produce a loud noise. 'Push in, push in, my darling,' cried Porphyry [the wife of one of his clerks] 'don't hold back! Thrust home as hard as you can; your pleasure will be the greater!' Hsi-men pulled her thighs wide apart and plunged furiously forward; while the woman, murmuring tremulously, fingered the stamen of her little flower.

Much of the work of Antoine Borel (1742–1810), French artist and engraver, was undisguised pornography. This plate, from a set of illustrations to an 18th-century French edition of *Fanny Hill* issued under a London imprint to protect the publisher's identity, is relatively restrained

5
Fun . . . and Trouble

It was through the eyes of Samuel Pepys that I became fascinated by the Restoration period in English history. Pepys whets the appetite, encouraging us to look more closely at what was accomplished in that thirty-year spell during the second half of the seventeenth century; much of the culture coming from the boundless talent in and on the fringe of the Stuart court. Of course, many played too hard and worked too little, so that the country might have foundered but for the energy and industry of less flamboyant personalities such as Pepys. But after the grey years of Cromwell, the inevitable lust for life, for colour, for diversion, for entertaining wit and conversation, resulted in an exhilarating upsurge in literature and the arts.

Many of these men had strong views, which they were not afraid to express forcibly, and often violently, but in general – apart from the enmity between Protestant and Catholic that eventually caused the downfall of James II – a live-and-let-live philosophy enabled people in all walks of life to broaden their horizons. Sex was a subject to be *enjoyed* and many of the great writers of the time had something to say on the subject.

Robert Herrick (1591–1674) has a place at the forefront of English pastoral poets, his love of nature and the countryside bequeathing such delightful classics as 'Cherry Ripe' and 'Gather Ye Rosebuds (While Ye May)'. A 'disciple' of Ben Jonson, Herrick became a clergyman – thrown out of his parish by the Puritans, but

---

(Opposite page, left) At the turn of the century, the French artist Paul Avril illustrated a number of erotic 'classics' such as *Portier des Chartreux*, an 18th-century account of naughty goings-on at a monastery, by Gervaise de Latouche. It was frequently reprinted in France but only occasionally translated into English. *(Right)* Cleland's internationally famous *Fanny Hill* was another book illustrated by Avril – here is a seldom reproduced poolside scene *(Courtesy of Bosworth Books)*

reinstated during the Restoration. Described as the 'most frankly pagan of English poets', Herrick's love of nature extended to this erotic pastoral scene. He called it 'The Vine':

I dream'd this mortal part of mine
Was Metamorphos'd to a Vine;
Which crawling one and every way,
Enthrall'd my dainty Lucia.
Me thought, her long small legs and thighs
I with my Tendrils did surprise;
Her Belly, Buttocks, and her Waist
By my soft Nerv'lets were embrac'd:
About her head I writhing hung,
And with rich clusters (hid among
The leaves) her temples I behung:
So that my Lucia seem'd to me
Young Bacchus ravisht by his tree.
My curles about her neck did crawl,
And arms and hands they did enthrall:
So that she could not freely stir,
(All parts there made one prisoner).
But when I crept with leaves to hide
Those parts, which maids keep unespy'd,
Such fleeting pleasures there I took,
That with the fancy I awoke;
And found (Ah me!) this flesh of mine
More like a Stock, than like a Vine.

On occasions he did not waste time beating about the bush, although the analogy with nature is still present in the poem 'Show Me Thy Feet'.

Show me those fleshy principalities; thy thighs,
Show me those fleshy principalities;
Show me that hill where smiling love doth sit,
Having a living fountain under it;
Show me thy waist, then let me therewithal,
By the assentation of thy lawn, see all.

The motley bunch of dissolute aristocrats who enjoyed the friendship of Charles II were but drinking and whoring companions; most of them, however, had the redeeming qualities of an appreciation of, and talent for producing, the written and spoken word. John Wilmot, second Earl of Rochester (1647–80), mentioned earlier, was unquestionably a writer of 'professional' standards, and one wonders what he might have achieved had circumstances forced on him a greater self-discipline. As we saw in Chapter 2, he was capable of shocking even blasé court circles, yet his poetry could be gentle, his words restrainedly evocative, as in the poem 'Beneath the Willows'. However, in comparison with Herrick, the style is clearly that of the man of experience and not that of a country parson:

As Chloris, full of harmless thought,
Beneath the willows lay,
Kind Love a comely shepherd brought
To pass the time away:
She blushed to be encountered so,
And chid the amorous swain;
But as she strove to rise and go,
He pulled her back again.

A sudden passion seized her heart
In spite of her disdain;
She found a pulse in every part,
And Love in every vein.
'Ah youth,' quoth she, 'what charms are these,
That conquer and surprise?
Ah let me – for, unless you please,
I have no power to rise.'

She faintly spoke and trembling lay,
For fear he should comply;
Her lovely eyes her heart betray,
And give her tongue the lie.
Thus she, who princes had denied
With all their pomp and train,
Was in the lucky minute tried
And yielded to the swain.

Somehow Rochester's poetry seems more in character when his mood is bitter. Graham Greene in *Lord Rochester's Monkey*, dealing with Rochester the politician, describes the inspiration for his 'Signor Dildoe'. Even in those days (1670) the Customs and Excise regarded it as their solemn duty to protect the public from itself, and had burned a consignment of dildoes. Rochester was asked to condemn the action, and typically his challenge took this form:

This Signor is sound, safe, ready and dumb,
As ever was candle, carrot or thumb;
Then away with the nasty devices and show
How you rate the just merit of Signor Dildoe.

In 'The Imperfect Enjoyment' both styles are evident, although the long poem really comes to life with the sudden injection of bitterness. The cause is impotence, more precisely the wilting of his penis at an inopportune moment:

Naked she lay, claspt in my longing arms,
I fill'd with love, and she all over charms,
Both equally inspir'd with eager fire,
Melting through kindness, flaming in desire;
With arms, legs, lips close clinging to embrace,
She clips me to her breast, and sucks me to her face.
The nimble tongue (love's lesser lightning) play'd
Within my mouth, and to my thoughts convey'd
Swift orders, that I should prepare to throw
The all-dissolving thunderbolt below.
My flutt'ring soul, sprung with the pointed kiss,
Hangs hov'ring o'er her balmy limbs of bliss.
But whilst her busy hand wou'd guide that part,
Which shou'd convey my soul up to her heart,
In liquid raptures I dissolve all o'er,
Melt into sperm and spend at every pore.
A touch from any part of her had don't,
Her hand, her foot, her very looks a –
Smiling, she chides in a kind murm'ring noise,
And sighs to feel the too hasty joys;
When, with a thousand kisses wand'ring o'er
My panting breast, and 'is there then no more?'
She cries: 'All this to love and rapture's due,
Must we not pay a debt to pleasure too?'
But I the most forlorn, lost man alive,
To shew my wisht obedience vainly swive,
I sigh alas! and kiss, but cannot drive.
Eager desires confound my first intent,

Succeeding shame does more success prevent,
And rage, at last, confirms me impotent.
Ev'n her fair hand, which might bid heat return
To frozen age, and make cold hermits burn,
Apply'd to my dead cinder, warms no more
Than fire to ashes cou'd past flames restore.
Trembling, confus'd, despairing, limber, dry,
A wishing, weak, unmoving lump I lie,
This dart of love, whose piercing point, oft try'd,
With virgin blood a hundred maids has dy'd,
Which nature still directed with such art,
That it through ev'ry port, reacht ev'ry heart,
Stiffly resolv'd, 'twould carelessly invade,
Woman or man, nor ought its fury staid;
Where e're it pierc'd, entrance it found or made –

Now languid lies, in this unhappy hour,
Shrunk up, and sapless, like a wither'd flow'r.
Thou treacherous, base, deserter of my flame,
False to my passion, fatal to my fame.
By what mistaken magic dost thou prove
So true to lewdness, so untrue to love?
What oyster – cinder – beggar – common whore,
Didst thou e're fail in all thy life before?
When vice, disease, and scandal led the way
With what officious haste didst thou obey?
Like a rude-roaring Hector in the streets
That scuffles, cuffs and ruffles all he meets;
But if his king or country claim his aid
The rascal villain shrinks and hides his head.
E'en so thy valour is displaid,
Breaks ev'ry stew, and does each small crack invade.
But if great Love the onset does command,
Base recreant to thy Prince, thou dost not stand.
Worst part of me, and henceforth hated most,
Through all the town the common rubbing post,
On whom each wretch relieves her lustful cunt,
As hogs, on gates, do rub themselves and grunt;
May'st thou to rav'nous shankers be a prey,
Or in continuous weepings waste away;
May stranguries and stone thy days attend;

May'st thou not piss, who didst refuse to spend,
When all my joys did on false thee depend.
And may ten thousand abler men agree
To do the wrong'd Corinna right for thee.

Of all the colourful personalities of the age, George Villiers, second Duke of Buckingham (1628–87) probably had the most drama and excitement in his life, even more than came to his famous father, the first Duke. Buckingham seemed to have a consuming determination to compete in, and win at, everything that took his fancy, and since love was one of those interests he did not hesitate to kill (in a duel) to win his mistress. As a political satirist, he conducted a vendetta with the greatest poet of the age, Dryden, although ultimately he came off second-best, and in due course Dryden was attacked and beaten up by 'unidentified' thugs. He was even jealous of his friend Rochester's success as a writer, and was another to demonstrate a remarkable flair of his own. He is remembered primarily in this context as a playwright, but his poetry was also of a high standard. His romantic verse includes 'To Celia':

Give, Celia, but to me alone
Ten thousand kisses all in one;
Let me not such from thee receive
As daughters to their fathers give,
Or as the sister to her brother,
Or the young fondling to her mother,
But such as by the panting bride,
Now lying at her husband's side;
(The fort but once or twice essayed
Not fully gained, still half a maid)
Are in sweet short breathed murmurs paid.
I must, to lengthen on the pleasure,
Dwell on thy lips, and kiss by leisure;
Who as not one that loves to kiss
Goddesses, breathless images,
Nor can I the most beauteous saint,
The loveliest face, salute in paint.
Warm flesh and blood I'd rather choose,
A tender creature full of juice,
Darting her nimble tongue between
My moistened lips; there meeting mine,

Sometimes I'd catch the pliant toy,
Suck it a while with eager joy;
Then let it go, and gently nip,
Instead of it the nether lip.

Thus Celia, would we sport away
Like cooing doves, the happy day;
And never sated with delight,
Begin the same again at night.
Compared with kisses such as these,
Nectar itself insipid is:
Give me but these alone, and leave
To stroke thy bubbies as they heave:
Let my hand thence, but quickly rove
Down to the pleasing seat of love,
Whither, do what we can, i'the end
Our curiosity will tend.

However, a poem entitled 'The Perfect Enjoyment' reproduced in some eighteenth-century collections of works by Rochester, his soulmate, is reckoned to have been penned by Buckingham, and indeed a footnote to an early edition maintains that he admitted authorship. What makes the poem particularly interesting is that it was probably composed as a jibe at 'The Imperfect Enjoyment'. Despite Rochester's cynicism, his work has a certain poignancy; Buckingham's 'perfect' state seems to echo the single mindedness of his philosophy:

Since now my Silvia is as kind as fair,
Let wit and joy succeed my dull despair.
O what a night of pleasure was the last!
A full reward for all my troubles past;
And on my head if future mischief fall
This happy night shall make amends for all.
Nay, though my Silvia's love should turn to hate,
I'll think of this, and die contented with my fate . . .

. . . Her hands at last, to hide her blushes, leave
The fort unguarded, willing to receive
My fierce assault, made with a lover's haste,
Like lightning piercing, and as quickly past.
Thus does fond nature with her children play;

Just shows us joy, then snatches it away
'Tis not the excess of pleasure makes it short;
The pain of love's as raging as the sport;
And yet, alas, that lasts; we sigh all night
With grief, but scarce one moment with delight.
Some little pain may check her kind desire,
But not enough to make her once retire;
Maids wounds for pleasure bear, as men for praise.

. . . Fond on the welcome guest, her arms embrace
My body, and her hands a better place,
Which with one touch so pleased and proud does grow
It swells beyond the grasp that made it so,
Confinement scorns in any straiter walls
Than those of love, where it contented falls.
Though twice o'er thrown, he more inflamed does rise
And will to the last drop fight our love's prize.
She like some Amazon in story proves,
That overcomes the hero whom she loves.
In the close strife she takes so much delight
She can then think of nothing but the fight.
With joy she lays him panting at her feet,
But with more joy does his recovery meet.
Her trembling hands first gently raise his head;
She almost dies for fear that he is dead;
Then binds his wounds up with a busy hand
And with that balm enables him to stand,
Till by her eyes she conquers him once more,
And wounds him deeper than she did before . . .

. . . At length all languishing and out of breath,
Panting as in the agonies of death,
We lie entranced, till one provoking kiss
Transports our ravished souls to paradise.
O heaven of love, thou moment of delight!
Wronged by my words; my fancy does thee right!
Methinks I lie all melting in her charms
And fast locked up within her legs and arms;
Bent are our minds, and all our thoughts on fire,
Just labouring in the pangs of fierce desire,
At once like misers wallowing in their store,
In full possession, yet desiring more.

Thus with repeated pleasures while we waste
Our happy hours, that like short minutes passed,
To such a sum of bliss our joys amount
The number now becomes too great to count.
Silent as night are all sincerest joys,
Like waters deepest running with least noise.
But now at last, for want of further force,
From deeds, alas we fall into discourse;
A fall which each of us in vain bemoans,
A greater fall than that of kings from thrones.
The tide of pleasure flowing now no more.
We lie like fish left gasping on the shore.
And now, as after fighting, wounds appear
Which we in heat did neither feel nor fear.
She for her sake entreats me to give o'er.
And yet for mine would gladly suffer more.
Her words are coy, while all her motions woo;
And when she asked me if it please me too,
I rage to show how well; but 'twill not do.
Thus would hot love run itself out of breath
And, wanting rest, find it too soon in death,
Did not wise nature with a gentle force
Refrain its rage, and stop its headlong course.
Indulgently severe, she well does spare
This child of hers, which most deserves her care.

Was it coincidence that another fair Sylvia was the heroine of an amusingly flippant piece by the master poet John Dryden (1631–1700), or could the girls be one and the same? There is just a possibility of that, in view of the enmity between Buckingham and Dryden, but to unravel the precise date of publication of the three pieces in question would require scholarly detective work.

Dryden, although regarded in his age as the greatest living poet, was not blessed with the creative genius of the other outstanding names in English literature, and his special talent (apart from his works of satire) lay in translating and often improving the words of others. Without the affluence of his contemporary rivals, he cold-bloodedly aspired to commercial success, writing what he thought the public wanted, although he was not always successful, as with a number of salacious plays which, in the main, did not earn the popularity enjoyed by other Restoration works. His outstanding translations included the works of Juvenal and Virgil, although after the overthrow of James II, when times were hard for him, he was sensible enough to turn his hand to material with wider potential sale – the erotic writings of Ovid, Boccaccio and Chaucer.

His song about the fair Sylvia was probably written at the time he was seeking public favour in the theatre, and hardly matches the image history has projected of the poet laureate:

Sylvia, the fair, in the bloom of fifteen,
Felt an innocent warmth as she lay on the green;
She had heard of a pleasure, and something she guest
By the towzing and tumbling, and touching her breast.

She saw the men eager, but was at a loss,
What they meant by their sighing, and kissing so close;
  By their praying and whining,
  And clasping and twining,
  And panting and wishing,
  And sighing and kissing,
And sighing and kissing so close.

Ah! she cried, ah, for a languishing maid,
In a country of Christians, to die without aid!
Not a Whig, or a Tory, or Trimmer at least,
Or a Protestant parson, or Catholic priest,
To instruct a young virgin, that is at a loss,
What they meant by their sighing and kissing so close!
  By their praying and whining
  And clasping and twining,
  And panting and wishing,
  And sighing and kissing,
And sighing and kissing so close.

Cupid, in shape of a swain, did appear,
He saw the sad wound, and in pity drew near;
Then showed her his arrow, and bid her not fear,
For the pain was no more than a maiden may bear.
When the balm was infused, she was not at a loss,
What they meant by their sighing, and kissing so close;
  By their praying and whining,
  And clasping and twining,

And panting and wishing,
And sighing and kissing,
And sighing and kissing so close.

All the writers mentioned in this chapter were men of some stature; none (with the exception of Rochester's misgivings on his deathbed) was embarrassed by dabbling in erotica. Perhaps the most celebrated man of the age was the great Frenchman Voltaire (1694–1778), who was respected in almost equal proportions for his genius as a philosopher, historian and playwright. Despite his constant battles with authority (he was banished from Paris in 1715, imprisoned in the Bastille two years later, and in due course exiled to England), his authority could never be ignored. Voltaire is best remembered today for the breadth of his political vision and his remarkably modern philosophy, and few of us know that his interests extended to sex and that he wrote about it in a delightfully amusing style in *La Pucelle d'Orléans*. With little respect for the reputation of national heroes, still less of divine intervention, Voltaire retold the story of Joan of Arc – except that he substituted sexual adventures indiscriminately every time he felt the story was slowing up; he wasn't going to bore his readers with dull chunks of history or even more tedious battles, when they could be having fun. Such was Voltaire's flair that at no time does the narrative descend to the repetitiveness of pornography. Voltaire's style reflected his belief in understatement. In fact, it was he who, in a very different context, warned against the peril of boring the reader with excess detail.

Another outstanding international figure was Benjamin Franklin (1706–90), although one has to admit that in England his name means relatively little, being vaguely associated with the American Declaration of Independence and the framing of the US constitution. By many Americans, however, he is respected not only as one of the nation's finest statesmen, but as a journalist-cum-publisher and scientific researcher (one of his many achievements being to identify lightning with electricity, and thus to introduce the use of lightning conductors on the tops of buildings).

Yet since most of his writing was of a political nature, it is not generally known that there was a less serious side to his character. In fact, his tongue-in-cheek erotic writing includes *Advice to a Young*

Man in Choosing a Mistress, produced in 1746 when he was post-master of Philadelphia. (How he would have turned in his grave at subsequent post-office interference with people's reading habits!) *A Letter to the Royal Academy at Brussels,* written some years later when he was in France (ably representing the newly formed United States), is scarcely erotic, being a pseudo-scientific discourse on the possibility of converting the odour of stomach wind into perfume by the addition of chemicals to one's food! Pleading that other famous inventions be put in perspective, the letter reads: 'And surely such a liberty of ex-pressing one's sentiments,* and pleasing one another, is of infinitely more importance to human happiness than that liberty of the press, or of abusing one another, which the English are so ready to fight and die for.'

Although it may not surprise many of us to hear that the remarkable Scottish poet, Robert Burns (1759–96), notorious philanderer and collector of erotica, had turned his talents to writing the stuff, most Burns scholars believe that the publishers of the erotic work associated with him merely used his name to boost sales. At the start of the nineteenth century, an anthology, anonymously edited, of eighty-five songs and poems, mostly of a sexual nature, was published under the title *The Merry Muses of Caledonia.* Among the intriguing titles were 'Nine Inch Will Please a Lady', 'A Hole To Hide It In', and 'Nae Hair On't'. Somehow, the rumour was spread – perhaps because of his reputation – that Burns was the author of some of them.

When the second edition was published in 1827, containing forty-two additions, the title-page read: '*The Merry Muses: A Choice Collection of Favourite Songs Gathered From Many Sources*, Compiled by Robert Burns including two of his letters and a poem Libel Summons never published before.' People merely assumed the rumours had been substantiated. A fascinating evaluation of the erotic works of Burns and their relationship to the *Merry Muses* is provided by Gershon Legman in *The Horn Book*, but the truth is still a matter for speculation.

* i.e., being able to fart pleasingly under the new order, to achieve a state in which 'the generous soul, who now endeavours to find out whether the friends he entertains like best claret or Burgundy, champagne or Madeira, would then enquire also whether they chose musk or lily, rose or bergamot, and provide accordingly'.

The most famous and certainly most successful piece of erotica ever published was *Memoirs of the Life of Fanny Hill, or the Memoirs of a Woman of Pleasure* (1748). The author (although it was originally published anonymously in two parts) was John Cleland, an English Foreign Office official down on his luck. It was written solely for money, and Cleland did quite well out of it, being paid 20 guineas – not bad for a little-known writer in the eighteenth century, although a drop in the ocean against the millions the book must have since earned, in hundreds of editions and in a variety of languages. His publisher, Ralph Griffiths, still under thirty when he brought out the book, is said to have earned £10,000 (worth about twenty times that amount today) in his lifetime, and that doesn't include a penny from the countless pirate editions that inevitably appeared. He sensibly cashed in on the success of Cleland, persuading him to write *Memoirs of a Coxcomb*, although compared with the earlier work it has the impact of a limp lettuce.

Although there is no bad language in *Fanny Hill*, its theme, that of an innocent country girl forced into prostitution and thus a succession of sexual adventures, before meeting true love and *living happily ever after* (!), alarmed the authorities, and Cleland was summoned before the Privy Council. Luckily the hearing was presided over by an enlightened Earl of Granville who recognised Cleland's true literary talent. When the author protested that he had merely written an exposé, a piece of crusading journalism, he was let off. In fact, the Earl gave him an annual pension of £100 on condition that he did not write anything of that sort again!

While *Fanny Hill* leaves little to the imagination, Cleland's language is always restrained. In the following short extract, Fanny is in her early days at the brothel and still innocent, although learning fast. From a hiding place she watches the 'Madam' entertaining a soldier:

> . . . he threw himself upon her, and his back being towards me, I could only take in his being ingulph'd for granted, by the directions he mov'd in, and the impossibility of missing so staring a mark; and now the bed shook, the curtains rattled so, that I could scarce hear the sighs and murmurs, the heaves and pantings, that accompanied the action, from the beginning to the end; the sound and sight of which thrill'd to the very soul of me, and made every

vein of my body circulate liquid fires: the emotion grew so violent that it almost intercepted my respiration.

Three years earlier, a fresh translation of a seventeenth-century French pornographic work, *The School of Venus*, was also prosecuted, and continued to be for some time. The writing was far more explicit than Cleland's and featured a conversation between (another) Fanny and Katy in which they luridly describe their sexual exploits. The book is far more pornographic than *Fanny Hill*, and thus would seem to offer 'better value' to the sensation seekers; yet *Fanny Hill* has survived as a classic of erotica and the other has disappeared.

Fanny Hill was harmless and even quite charming in places, and the authorities reacted sensibly; but then, they did not have to contend with pressures or interference from outside. When such 'pressures' are political, even routine objections can be whipped up into hysteria. The English politician John Wilkes (1727–97), a man whose strong views earned the hatred of his opponents, suffered the consequences of such harassment. Wilkes happened to run a private press; in 1762 he founded *The North Briton* and in the following year was arrested for libel after one issue had accused the King of lying in a speech. He was found guilty but pleaded parliamentary privilege. Yet he barely had time to catch his breath before his printing activities again landed him in hot water. This time it was a pretty outrageous long poem entitled 'An Essay on Woman'. The run was limited to thirteen copies, but apparently an employee made an extra copy which got into the hands of a political enemy, the Earl of Sandwich.

The House of Lords issued a warrant for his arrest, declaring the essay was 'a most scandalous, obscene, and impious libel, a gross profanation of many parts of the Holy Scriptures, and a most wicked and blasphemous attempt to ridicule and vilify the person of our Blessed Saviour'. Wilkes sensibly moved to the Continent. Although, as usual at that time, the sexual content was less upsetting to his contemporaries than the blasphemy, Wilkes (had he stopped to argue) would not have been helped by a drawing of a large penis beneath the title, and a lewd frontispiece depicting 'The Saviour of the World'. The following extract is a typical example of what upset his critics, but the style, despite the explicit terms, would raise relatively few eyebrows today:

Heaven from all creatures hides the Book of Fate
All but the page prescribed, the present state,
From boys what girls, from girls what women know
Or what could suffer being here below?
Thy lust the Virgin dooms to bleed today:
Had she thy reason would she skip and play?
Pleased to the last, she likes the luscious food,
And grasps the prick just raised to shed her blood.
Oh! Blindness to the Future, kindly given,
That each may enjoy what fucks are mark'd by Heaven.
Who sees with equal Eye, as God of all,
The Man just mounting, and the Virgin's fall;
Prick, cunt, and bollocks in convulsions hurl'd,
And now a Hymen burst and now a world.
Hope, humbly then, clean girls; nor vainly soar;
But fuck the cunt at hand, and God adore.
What future fucks he gives not thee to know,
But gives that Cunt to be thy blessing now.

How much of the outrage was genuine and how much manufactured by Wilkes' enemies is not known. Although he was something of a debauchee, he certainly did not write the poem, the authorship of which has never been determined. Just over a hundred years later, the magazine *Fortnightly Review* advanced the theory that it was written by the son of the then Archbishop of Canterbury!

Wilkes' enormous popularity got him elected to Parliament again after a four-year exile (only to be expelled again in 1769 for another libel!), and still again. He even became Lord Mayor of London. One of his major contributions to British politics was to secure the right of the press to attend parliamentary debates.

A contemporary of Wilkes and a more likeable person was the Italian adventurer Giovanni Giacomo Casanova, Chevalier de Seingalt (1725–98), who spent most of his life travelling Europe as a journalist, diplomat and spy, but always finding time to indulge in his principal hobby – seduction. Casanova was intended for the church, but expelled from the seminary while still in his teens for immoral conduct. His travels having taken him to France, Switzerland, Poland, Spain and England, he didn't get round to writing his memoirs until the last few years of his life. The memoirs were first published in France in twelve volumes between 1826 and 1838, but remained in expurgated form until this century. This is somewhat surprising since, like Cleland before him, Casanova's language is discreet and would not in itself cause offence, although in 1797 he wrote 'those whose favourite virtue is chastity . . . had better refrain from reading me'.

However, since he was also writing what amounted to a social document of his time, dealing with the early use of modern contraceptives and sex aids, it was presumably felt that such brazenness presented a threat to public morality. In one lighthearted love-making incident with an enthusiastic nun, he produces a contraceptive, 'a little article of transparent skin, about eight inches long, with one opening, which was ornamented with a red rosette', which she puts on for him:

> 'There you are [she says] hooded like a mother abbess, but in spite of the fineness of the sheath I like the little fellow better quite naked. I think that this covering degrades us both.'
>
> 'You are right, it does. But let us not dwell on these ideas, which will only spoil our pleasure.'
>
> 'We will enjoy our pleasure directly; let me be reasonable now, for I have never thought of these matters before. Love must have invented these little sheaths, but it must first have listened to the voice of prudence, and I do not like to see love and prudence allied.'
>
> 'The correctness of your argument surprises me, but we will philosophize another time.'
>
> 'Wait a minute. I have never seen a man before, and I have never wished to enjoy the sight as much as now. Ten months ago, I should have called this article an invention of the devil; but now I look upon the inventor as a benefactor. . . . But tell me, how is it that the makers of these things remain unmolested; I wonder that they are not found out, excommunicated, or heavily fined, or even punished corporally, if they are Jews as I expect. Dear me, the makers of this one must have measured you badly! Look! it is too large here, and too small there; it makes you into a regular curve. What a stupid fellow he must be, he can't know his own trade! But what is that?'

That, Casanova is not too pompous to admit, was the consequence of

The illustrations of Emil Sartori for the 1910 French edition of the frequently reprinted *La Bonbonnière* had a haunting fairytale quality to their eroticism. A German edition of this book published two years earlier was illustrated by von Bayros (*Courtesy Bosworth Books*)

all that talk and handling, and he is obliged to replace the contraceptive with another that, incidentally, fitted rather better.

No book or anthology dealing with sex literature could omit the Marquis de Sade (1740–1814), but his writings are the products of a sick mind – scarcely in the category of good healthy erotica. It may be possible to relate sadism to sex in an erotic style (*The Story of O*, for example), but there is a disgusting quality about de Sade; he did spend a fair proportion of his life in prison for offences that included causing death through the administration of powerful purges, and eventually died in a lunatic asylum.

The two books with which he is especially identified are *Justine* (1791) and *Juliette* (a companion volume), which relate the adventures of penniless sisters in an inhospitable world. In the first, the virtuous Justine has to contend with not only relatively respectable murderers, but Satanists, pederasts and vampires, while in the other book Juliette – who, having failed to beat the system, joins it – takes up with characters indulging in cannibalism and coprophagy.

Literary forgery sometimes throws up talent on a par with the writer emulated, or sometimes greater, as in the case of Thomas Chatterton (1752–70). There is often less concern with establishing the authenticity of the 'newly discovered' piece, when it is a minor work, especially when it is in doubtful taste and the copied master had something of a notorious reputation, as in the case of Robert Burns or Lord Byron (1788–1824). In such situations mud sticks easily, especially when the slandered person is dead. Among the many great works of Byron was his poem of ideas and morals, *Don Juan*, produced in 'instalments' between 1819 and 1824. It was this 'peg' that presumably encouraged someone to write a long poem, *Don Leon*, a 1,455 line defence of sodomy, and the companion poem, *Leon*

(Opposite page, left) The romantic style of the German artist Franz von Bayros (1866–1924) made him much in demand as a book illustrator and to design collector's bookplates. He often used the pseudonym Choisy le Conin. He added an extra dimension to many of the classics, including *Fanny Hill*, Murger's *Bohème* and Aretino's *Sonnets*. This is from *The Pretty Andalusian* by Francisco Delicado, Spain's erotic classic *(Courtesy of Bosworth Books)*. *(Right)* This delicate hand-coloured plate has never been catalogued but is believed to be the work of Berthommé St André, probably done for one of the several Pierre Louys books he illustrated. Most of his best work was done from the turn of the century to the 1930s *(Courtesy of Bosworth Books)*

to Annabella, publishing them in Byron's name sixty-two years after the poet's death. In the first, the writer suggests that Byron practised sodomy on his wife when she was pregnant.

I burn to press thee, but I fear to try,
Lest like an incubus my weight should lie;
Lest, from the close encounter we should doom
Thy quickening foetus to an early tomb.
Thy size repels me, whilst thy charms invite;
Then, say, how celebrate the marriage rite?
Learn'd Galen, Celsus, and Hippocrates,
Have held it good, in knotty points like these,
Lest mischief from too rude assaults should come,
To copulate ex more pedudum.
What sayst thou, dearest? Do not cry me nay;
We cannot err where science shows the way,
She answered not; but silence gave consent,
And by that threshold boldly in I went.
So clever statesmen, who concoct by stealth
Some weighty measures for the commonwealth,
All comers by the usual door refuse,
And let the favoured few the back stairs use.

It was only after many years, and several pirate reprints, that Byron scholars rejected the poems.

In a different vein, Gilbert and Sullivan were for many years suspected of having written *The Sod's Opera*, with characters such as Count Tostoff, the brothers Bollox, a pair of hangers-on, and Scrotum, a wrinkled old retainer. In fact, the opera is described and elaborated upon in several books, although Legman once again spoils everyone's fun in *The Horn Book* by establishing that such an opera doesn't exist. He points out that the legend grew around something slightly similar from the pen of George Augustus Sala – which, let's face it, doesn't sound half as interesting.

In this cursory view of erotic literature in history, I have been obliged to omit dozens of interesting or curious titles, many highly pornographic but with few pretensions to literature. A woman wrote one of the better-known pornographic books of the nineteenth century, and it is worth a final diversion to include her, not so much on merit, but for the novelty of the advertisements included in the four volumes. The book, published in 1824, was *The Voluptarian Cabinet*, and the author's pseudonym was Mary Wilson, not a writer but the proprietor of a London brothel. The stories did at least have an element of authenticity, but I find the notes and advertisements far more entertaining than the very routine stories:

> In the area between the two rows of houses I have erected a most elegant temple, in the centre of which are large saloons, entirely surrounded with boudoirs most elegantly and commodiously fitted up. In these saloons, according to their classes, are to be seen the finest men of their species I can procure, occupied in whatever amusements are adapted to their taste, and all kept in a high state of excitement by good living and idleness.
>
> The ladies will never enter the saloons even in their masks, but view their inmates from a darkened window in each boudoir. In one they will see fine elegantly dressed young men, playing at cards, music etc – in others athletic men, wrestling or bathing, in a state of perfect nudity – in short they will see such a variety of the animal, that they cannot fail of suiting their inclinations. Having fixed upon one she would like to enjoy, the lady has only to ring for the chambermaid, call her to the window, point out the object, and he is immediately brought to the boudoir. She can enjoy him in the dark, or having a light, or keep on her mask. She can stay an hour or a night, and have one or a dozen men as she pleases, without being known to any of them. A lady of 70 or 80 years of age can at pleasure enjoy a fine robust youth of 20; and to elevate the mind to the sublimest raptures of love, every boudoir is surrounded with the most superb paintings of Aretino's *Postures* after Julio Romano and Ludovico Carracci, interspersed with large mirrors, also a side-board covered with the most delicious viands and richest wines. The whole expense of the institution is defrayed by a subscription from each lady of one hundred guineas per annum, with the exception of the refreshments which are to be paid for at the time. . . .
>
> The greatest possible pains have been taken to preserve order and regularity and it is impossible that any discovery can take place by the intrusion of police or enraged cuckolds, as will be demonstrated before . . . Having thus made it my study to serve my own sex in a most essential point, I trust to their liberality for encouragement in my arduous undertaking; and am, Ladies, your most obedient Servant, MARY WILSON.

6
Darkest Before The Dawn (1850–1950)

Irrespective of Society's changing attitudes, the watchdogs of morality are guaranteed to be consistent in one thing: their *in*consistency. Hard porn tends to slip through unnoticed while they are preoccupied with a work of art. The case of Walt Whitman (1819–92), one of America's best-loved poets, is typical. Whitman possessed the talent and originality to make his mark in any age, but at the halfway stage of the nineteenth century his freedom of form and expression was a radical departure from accepted rhyme and metre. That created problems enough.

But Whitman was a rebel in other ways, and displayed considerable moral courage in the face of widespread criticism of the style and *content* of his poetry. By the time he published a thin volume of twelve of his own poems, *Leaves of Grass* (1855), he was a successful Brooklyn journalist. The style immediately earned praise from certain literary critics, but criticism elsewhere in equal measure. A year later, a publisher was found for an enlarged edition, although some of the new poems proved too outspoken for him, and he returned the entire print run to Whitman. Apart from the confusing new style, the critics objected to some of the direct references to homosexuality, but Whitman stuck to his guns and refused to withdraw. The attitude to such pressures is summed up in his comment: 'The dirtiest book in all the world is an expurgated book.'

The anthology, widely read after many editions in the United States, is less known in Europe. Here are two of the poems; the first from 'I Sing The Body Electric' dealing with heteorosexual love:

Hair, bosom, hips, bend of legs, negligent falling hands,
all diffused – mine too diffused;

Ebb stung by the flow, and flow stung by the ebb –
love-flesh swelling and deliciously aching;
Limitless limpid jets of love hot and enormous, quivering
jelly of love, white-blow and delicious juice;
Bridegroom night of love, working surely and
softly into the prostrate dawn . . . .

The second, from 'Whoever You Are, Holding Me Now in Hand' has a homosexual theme:

Or possibly with you sailing at sea, or on the beach of
the sea, or some quiet island,
Here to put your lips upon mine I permit you,
With the comrade's long-dwelling kiss, or the new
husband's kiss,
For I am the new husband, and I am the comrade.

But the prejudice with which Whitman had to contend was mild compared to the harrassment in England of the publisher, Henry Vizetelly, a scholarly man who was accused of what might have passed as conspiring to soil the minds of Englishmen. His crime was to publish the works of Emile Zola, a contemptible muck-raker and a foreigner to boot! He should have been warned, I suppose, because in 1880 the *Methodist Times* had attacked even Henry James for praising Zola, declaring: 'Zolaism is a disease. It is a study of the putrid. Even France has shown signs that she has had enough of it. No one can read Zola without moral contamination.'

Having published a wide selection of 'respectable' material, Vizetelly began issuing translations of Zola's work in 1884, lightly expurgated for the more delicate English taste. Four years later he was prosecuted for a translation of *La Terre* (*Earth* or *The Soil*, depending on the translator), and fined £100 for what was described as a 'brutal obscenity'. A year later he had obviously not learned the error of his ways and he was prosecuted again over other books – five by Zola and two by Guy de Maupassant – and although now seventy years old and ill, he was sent to prison for three months. He died in 1894, largely as a result of the strain.

Vizetelly having been 'put in his place' by society, there followed a typical example of Victorian double standards. The publishers Chatto & Windus took over Zola's titles in the United Kingdom and issued them, heavily expurgated; yet between 1894 and 1895, six of the novels were *privately* printed in unexpurgated form, without any fuss.

Feelings ran high over the Vizetelly case and it is worth recalling the opposing points of view. The first, from a leader in the London *Times* of 1 November 1888, scarcely conforms to the romanticised image of *The Thunderer*, which has always claimed to epitomise the highest standards of impartial journalism. It read:

> Between prudery and pruriency in such matters there is a wide debatable ground, and it is not always easy to draw the line which separates what is permissable from what is not. But if the line is not to be drawn so as to exclude translations of such works of Zola as *La Terre* and *Pot Bouille* it is plain that it cannot be drawn at all. Other French works of fiction published in translation by Mr Vizetelly, such as the novels of Gaboriau and du Boisgobey, are not always very healthy reading; but their main interest lies in the elucidation of mystery or in the play of intrigue, and not in mere and sheer obscenity, naked, shameless and utterly vile. . . . We cannot but rejoice, therefore, that Mr Vizetelly has acknowledged his offence and been punished for it.

The comparison is interesting because the works in question are so very different. Émile Gaboriau (1835–73) and Fortuné du Boisgobey (1824–91) wrote mere pot-boilers compared with Zola, although it must be said that Gaboriau was a trend-setter among thriller writers.

The second view is an extract from Vizetelly's letter to the Treasury's Solicitor, Sir A. K. Stephenson, KCB, in 1888:

> England may render itself ridiculous in the eyes of Europe by visiting the works of M. Zola with the same kind of condemnation which the civilized world has accorded to the writings of the degraded Marquis de Sade; still it requires no particular foresight to predict that a couple of generations hence, when the tribe of prejudiced scribes – who, ignorant for the most part of their own country's literature [This was a reference to the eroticism in English classics freely available] now join in the hue and cry against M. Zola – are relegated to their proper obscurity, the works of the author of the Rougon-Macquart family, (in) spite of their admitted coarseness, will rank as classics among the production of the great writers of the past.

Zola was, admittedly, interested in the more sordid features of people and life, but the tremendous power and virility of his writing mentioned earlier, is undeniable. Many of his books contain passages that are distinctly erotic, yet it is not this to which his critics objected so much as the general *unpleasantness* of the stories. Life may be nasty, but one does one's best not to draw attention to it. The sweeping of unpleasantness under the carpet reminds me of a Russian friend who, defending the persecution of dissident writers, said to me, 'There are so many nice things to write about, why must they pick on unpleasant themes?' Of course, many saw no merit in Zola's work at all; it was even called 'inartistic garbage' (*Society*, 21 April 1888).

It is interesting to reflect that while Zola got the English so hot under the collar, he was accepted without question in America, while the reverse is true of Whitman.

Meanwhile, literature more directly linked with sex, particularly the underground variety, was enjoying a boom. In England there was a special demand for establishments catering for mild sadism and masochism, and dozens of pornographic books soon followed the fashion – pornographic in the sense that no proper storyline was allowed to interfere with the continuous detailed description of flagellation, usually of delectable young ladies. Vocabulary was limited and almost unnecessary beyond a few key adjectives, including 'inflamed' (referring to bare bottoms) and 'flashing' (which could describe eyes or whips – although written today would convey something very different!)

The word 'masochism' was coined by the psychologist Krafft-Ebing after Leopold von Sacher-Masoch (1836-95), who 'popularised' a long-established fetish in 1870 with his semi-autobiographical long short story *Venus in Furs*, which has become acknowledged as a masterpiece of its genre. While the style is reasonably literate, and relatively inoffensive, there is really little to justify the book's place in the history of erotic literature.

As the title suggests, the story concerns a young man, Severin, obsessed with being beaten by his beautiful mistress, particularly when she is naked apart from her furs. Although the concept of being whipped until the blood flows is distateful to many of us, Sacher-Masoch's style is restrained. In the following passage the translation is by George Warner. Severin, having contracted to serve as Wanda's servant, is regularly ill-treated and is eventually humiliated when she takes another lover, a sadistic Greek:

Why does my heart beat so? I am still very happy

I opened the door slowly and drew the curtain aside. There lies Wanda on the sofa, pretending not to see me. How beautiful she looks in her gray silk dress which admirably displays her figure and leaves her throat and arms uncovered. Her hair is tied with a red velvet ribbon. A bright fire burns on the hearth, and the lamp floods the room with blood-red rays.

'Wanda!' said I at last.

'Oh, Severin!' exclaimed she joyously. 'I have been longing for you to come.' She got up quickly and flung her arms round me; then she sat down and drew me to her, but I slipped quietly to her feet and rested my head in her lap. 'Do you know. I am very much in love with you today,' whispered she; then, pushing my hair back, she kissed my eyes. 'How beautiful your eyes are! I've always loved them, but never more than today. I could die for them.' She stretched out her adorable limbs, and enveloped me with a soft look from her own half-closed eyes. 'But how cold you are'. You hold me as though I were a piece of wood. Wait a bit, I will make you love me.' Once more she hung on my eyes in a wheedling, caressing way. 'I don't please you any longer. I must still be cruel to you. I have been too nice to you today, I can see. I tell you what, my little madman, I am going to flog you a bit.'

'But, child'

'I want to.'

'Wanda!'

'Come on, let me tie you up. I want to see you in love again. Here's the rope . . . if only I can manage it'

With that, she began to tie my feet, and then she fastened my hands behind my back as though I were a criminal.

'That's it! Can you move?'

'No.'

'Right!'

She made a loop in one of the ropes and slipped it over my head and down to my hips, and then fastened me to the bedpost. A strange shiver passed through me. 'I feel like a martyr,' I said.

'Yes, you're going to be really whipped today.'

'I should like you to put your fur coat on.'

'I don't mind doing that for you,' said she, putting on her fur and then standing with folded arms in front of me and looking at me with half-closed eyes. 'Do you remember the tale of Denys's bull?'

'Not very well. What is it?'

'A courtier invented for the tyrant a new kind of torture, a brass bull in which the victim was placed, and then a fire lit underneath. As soon as the bull began to get hot, the victim began to howl, and his cries were like the bellowing of a bull. Denys smiled graciously on the inventor and, to test the invention, had him shut up in the bull. There is much to be learnt from that tale. You have taught me pride and cruelty and egotism, and you shall be my first victim. I find real pleasure in having in my power a man who thinks, feels, and wills as I; who is stronger in mind and body than I; and who loves me in spite of my behaviour. Do you still love me?'

'With all my heart.'

'That's all right then, and you will get all the more pleasure from what I am going to do with you.'

'What's the matter with you? I don't understand you. Your eyes are ablaze with cruelty today, and you are strangely beautiful . . . Venus in furs, incarnate!'

Without replying, Wanda put her arm round my neck and kissed me, and all my being surged with mad passion.

'But where is the whip?'

Wanda smiled and stepped back.

'So you really want to be flogged?' asked she, disdainfully throwing back her head.

'Yes.'

Then Wanda's expression changed completely. Her face was drawn with anger and she seemed hateful to me at that moment.

'All right, whip him!' cried she aloud.

And then the handsome Greek pushed his curly head through the bed-hangings. I was struck dumb with surprize. The situation was downright comic; I could have laughed like mad if it hadn't been so desperately sad and shameful for me.

This went beyond my dream. A cold shiver ran down my back when my rival advanced with his riding boots, his tight white breeches and close-fitting jacket, and when my eyes took in his athletic form.

'You are cruel to this point?' asked he of Wanda.

'Only for the pleasure it brings. Life is nothing without pleasure. The one who enjoys life doesn't want to die, while those who suffer look on death as a friend. But those who are out to enjoy life must take it in the ancient sense: they must not be afraid to plunge into debauchery even at another's expense . . . Men who want to live like Olympian gods must have slaves to throw to the lions, and gladiators at their feasts who will fight to death.'

Her words pierced my soul through and through. I understood perfectly.

'Untie me!' I shouted furiously.

'Aren't you my slave, my property?' demanded Wanda, 'or must I show you the contract?'

'Untie me!' I cried threateningly, 'or else . . .'

'Can he get loose?' asked Wanda, 'for he has already menaced my life.'

'You needn't bother,' said the Greek as he examined my bonds.

'I shall shout for help.'

'No one will hear you, and no one shall prevent me from profaning once more your most sacred sentiments and behaving in a downright frivolous way,' continued she, contemptuously quoting the words of my letter to her. 'Do you think I am now cruel and pitiless, or am I on the way to becoming vulgar? What! do you still love me? . . . or do you hate and despise me? Here's the whip . . .' and she handed it to the Greek, who sprang up to me.

'Don't you dare hit me,' I cried, trembling with anger. 'I'll stand nothing from you.'

'You say that because I'm not wearing furs,' replied the Greek, grinning, and picking up Wanda's zibeline.

'You're very good,' said Wanda, giving him a kiss and helping him with the coat.

'Must I really flog him?'

'Do what you like with him.'

'Brute!' I hissed.

The Greek eyed me savagely and tried the whip. His muscles swelled as he cracked it in the air. As for me, I am bound like Marsyus and condemned to see Apollo himself skin me alive.

My eyes wandered round the room and rested on the counterpane representing Samson having his eyes thrust out by the Philistines what time he lies at Delilah's feet. The picture seemed to me to be a symbol, like the eternal allegory of passion, volupty and love which woman inspires in man. Each of us becomes a Samson in the bud and is foully betrayed by the woman he loves, whether she be dressed in cloth or fur.

'Now, watch me tame him,' said the Greek.

He bared his teeth, and a blood-thirsty look came over his face, such as I had seen when I first met him.

And then he began to flog me so unmercifully, so frightfully, that I shivered at every blow and trembled from head to foot with pain. Tears poured down my cheeks while Wanda, reclining on the sofa, contemplated this scene with cruel curiosity and laughing the while.

It is impossible to describe the feelings of a man when he is being ill-treated by the man whom his beloved prefers. I was ready to die with shame and despair.

What is most ignominious is that, in my painful situation, under the whip of Apollo and the laughter of my cruel Venus, I felt at first a sort of ultra-sensual fantastic charm. But the whip soon dissipated all the charm; the blows rained on me so thick and fast that, able to stand no more, I clenched my teeth and away faded dream, and woman, and love.

I then realized with terrible precision that, since Holofernes and Agamemnon, blind passion and volupty have always been man's ruin, and have brought him to misery, slavery, and death.

I felt as though I were waking from a dream.

My blood was now flowing freely under the whip, and I twisted and turned like a trodden worm; but he kept on striking and she kept on laughing and showing no pity. Meanwhile, she packed her trunks, and then, still laughing, got in the carriage which stood waiting at the door.

Then all sound ceased.

I listened, holding my breath.

The carriage rattled, the horses sped away, and all was over . . .

Charles Baudelaire (1821–67) and Algernon Swinburne (1837–1909) were among the distinguished writers who tried their hand at describing the 'pleasures' of flagellation. Swinburne provoked an outburst of hysteria with his *Poems and Ballads* (1866), but Baudelaire, recognised as one of the outstanding poets of the French Romantic movement, got into hotter water with his greatest work *Les Fleurs du Mal* (1857). He and his publisher were actually prosecuted because of the 'impropriety' of some of the poems. Poetry by its very nature does not lend itself to pornography as readily as prose in a fetish as sterile as this. With the exception of *The Story of O* (discussed later), which does at least try to get into the minds of its heroine and the men she allows to dominate her, I find this type of literature tedious. However, enthusiasts should read Luke Rhinehart's *The Dice Man* for one long sequence of sex and violence which is at once terrifyingly real, funny, erotic and always brilliantly written.

Only a handful of writers throughout history have possessed the genius capable of influencing literature to the extent of changing the accepted pattern. A larger number have been considered 'ahead of their time' and have set trends (Walt Whitman, for example), but seldom has anyone made the impact of James Joyce (1882-1941) whose *Ulysses* (Paris, 1922) created as much controversy in literary circles as the exploding of the first atom bomb made on society generally a quarter of a century later.

Ulysses had first appeared in the New York literary journal *The Little Review* in 1918, continuing in monthly instalments over the next three years. The Society for the Suppression of Vice instigated a prosecution at one stage and the publisher was fined $100. The notoriety resulted in a number of pirated editions which earned money for a lot of people – except, as is always the case, the author. He eventually found a genuine publisher in Paris, and in 1922 the book appeared – in itself something of a feat. The French typesetters knew little English, and not only was Joyce's English strange enough to English eyes, but the manuscript was in his almost incomprehensible handwriting. On top of these headaches, Joyce's eyesight was failing, and he had difficulty in reading the proofs – 700 pages of them.

However, after that monumental task had been accomplished, the newly published masterpiece immediately ran into fresh problems, 500 copies being burned by the United States Department of Posts, and a similar number by His Majesty's Customs as they entered Folkestone. Yet before long it was being hailed as a work of genius; it was put on the English literature reading list at Harvard by T. S. Eliot in 1932 – two years before the ban was raised in the United States by an enlightened judge, a decision that prepared the way for its eventual publication in the United Kingdom in 1939.

Eight out of ten of the people who rushed to buy *Ulysses* because of its reputation must have been mystified and frustrated by the author's style, or rather, his conglomerate of writing styles, and even more so by his use of strange polysyllabic creations such as *contransmagnificandjewbangtantially, honorificabilitunidinitatibus* and *eppripfftaph*. (The book seems like a nursery-school easy-reader, however, when compared with *Finnegan's Wake*, published in 1939.) The more industrious of the shabby-raincoat brigade had to settle for passages like this extract:

> . . . he fell in with a certain whore of an eyepleasing exterior whose name, she said, is Bird-in-the-Hand and she beguiled him wrongways from the true path by her flatteries that she said to him as, Ho, you pretty man, turn aside hither and I will show you a brave place, and she lay at him so flatteringly that she had him in her grot which is named Two-in-the-Bush, or, by some learned, Carnal Concupiscence . . . for that foul plague Allpox and the monsters they cared not for them, for Preservative had given them a stout shield of oxengut and, third, that they might take no hurt neither from Offspring that was that wicked devil by virtue of this same shield which was named Killchild.

The style of Joyce is eulogised by Anthony Burgess in the London *Observer* magazine (20 July 1979), in an essay outlining why *Ulysses* is one of his favourite novels: 'Joyce is candid about the dullness, and his substitute for exciting events is the excitement of a variable prose-style that is almost hysterically responsive to the content of what it has to describe.' He goes on to describe the style as 'opaque or iridescent', 'imitating a symphony or a political poster . . . literature is made out of language, and that language should be glorified, not made servile and near invisible as in a novel by . . .' (he goes on to be rude about other writers, but that's irrelevant to our topic).

I was intrigued to learn that Dr Hans Gabler of the University of Munich, West Germany, is currently engaged (at least, well into the 1980s) in producing the first definitive edition of Ulysses – with the aid of a computer. Because of the difficulties mentioned, he estimates that the Paris edition contained about two thousand errors, most of them compounded in future imprints. Dr Gabler and his assistants feed the various versions into the computer, which analyses them, makes exhaustive comparisons and rejects what it regards as errors. With more than a million words to sift, Dr Gabler says that without the computer the task would have taken fifteen years.

James Branch Cabell (1879–1958) was another fine novelist who fell foul of the moralists with *Jurgen*. Cabell chose to treat his critics with disdain, refusing even to defend the book; fortunately there were many others who did that for him. The plot – a magic shirt given to our hero, Jurgen, making him irresistible (in his various guises) to the remarkable women he meets – was enough to make some people assume it must be a dirty book. In fact, *Jurgen* is a delightful blend of fantasy, popular legend and history, written in a gently humorous style that would not bring a blush to the cheek of the proverbial maiden aunt. And on the subject of blushes, the following passage surely makes my point. Jurgen is bent on seduction, but, oh, how courteously! His adversary is the beautiful Yolande, Lady of the Green Castle, who begins by reproaching him:

> 'Oh, but how stupid it is of you, Messire de Logreus, to stand there grinning and looking at me in a way that makes me blush!'
>
> 'Well, that is easily remedied,' said Jurgen, as he blew out the candles, 'since women do not blush in the dark.'
>
> 'What do you plan, Messire de Logreus?'
>
> 'Ah, do not be alarmed!' said Jurgen. 'I shall deal fairly with you.'
>
> And in fact Yolande confessed afterward that, considering everything, Messire de Logreus was very generous. Jurgen confessed nothing: and as the room was profoundly dark nobody else can speak with authority as to what happened there. It suffices that the Duke of Logreus and the Lady of the Green Castle parted later on the most friendly terms.
>
> 'You have undone me, with your games and your candles and your scrupulous returning of courtesies,' said Yolande, and yawned, for she was sleepy; 'but I fear that I do not hate you as much as I ought to.'
>
> 'No woman ever does,' says Jurgen, 'at this hour.'

Fantasy and the legends of different lands irretrievably entangled, Jurgen meets and falls in love with Guinevere (the wife of King Arthur). At one point Cabell describes her beauty through Jurgen's eyes in the traditional Romantic style, at times trite but effective.

> The head of Guenevere [*sic*], be it repeated, was small: you wondered at the proud free tossing movements of that little head which had to sustain the weight of so much hair. The face of Guenevere was coloured tenderly and softly: it made the faces of other women seem the work of a sign-painter, just splotched in

> anyhow. Grey eyes had Guenevere, veiled by incredibly long black lashes that curved incredibly. Her brows arched rather high above her eyes: that was almost a fault. Her nose was delicate and saucy: her chin was impudence made flesh: and her mouth was a tiny and irresistible temptation.

But the author's special charm is that he never takes himself too seriously. Jurgen's daydreams are quickly followed by this more down-to-earth reflection:

> 'And so on, and so on! But indeed there is no sense at all in describing this lovely girl as though I were taking an inventory of my shop-window,' said Jurgen. 'Analogues are all very well, and they have the unanswerable sanction of custom: none the less, when I proclaim that my adored mistress's hair reminds me of gold I am quite consciously lying. It looks like yellow hair, and nothing else: nor would I willingly venture within ten feet of any woman whose head sprouted with wires, of whatever metal. And to protest that her eyes are as grey and fathomless as the sea is very well also, and the sort of thing which seems expected of me: but imagine how horrific would be puddles of water slopping about in a lady's eye-sockets! If we poets could actually behold the monsters we rhyme of, we would scream and run. Still, I rather like this sirvente.'

Time stands still for Jurgen, in common with most heroes of fantasy, but where have you seen such an appealing account?

> So it was that Jurgen came into Cocaigne, wherein is the bedchamber of Time. And Time, they report, came in with Jurgen, since Jurgen was mortal: and Time, they say, rejoiced in this respite from the slow toil of dilapidating cities stone by stone, and with his eyes tired by the finicky work of etching in wrinkles, went happily into his bed-chamber, and fell asleep just after sunset on this fine evening in late June: so that the weather remained fair and changeless, with no glaring sun rays anywhere, and with one large star shining alone in clear daylight. This was the star of Venus Mechanitis, and Jurgen later derived considerable amusement from noting how this star was trundled about the dome of heaven by a largish beetle, named Khepre. And the trees everywhere kept their first fresh foliage, and the birds were about their indolent evening songs, all during Jurgen's stay in Cocaigne, for Time had

gone to sleep at the pleasantest hour of the year's most pleasant season. So tells the tale.

In the 1930s there were countless examples of respectable books being dragged through the dirt long after publication, typical cases of locking the stable-door after the horse has bolted. However, in 1932 Geoffrey de Montalk was actually sent to prison for six months on a charge of uttering an obscene libel *before* his poems were published. Whether, like John Wilkes a couple of hundred years before, de Montalk, a Polish count with pretensions to the Polish throne, was harassed by police for political ends is difficult to determine, but he was described by police at the Old Bailey, not as a good or bad writer but as 'an agitator'.

The Count had produced a manuscript with three poems for a printer, who decided to hand it to the police. One of the poems was 'Here Lies John Penis':

Here lies John Penis
Buried in the Mount of Venus.
He died in tranquil faith
That having vanquished death
He shall rise up again
And in Joy's Kingdom reign.

Meanwhile, in 1931, a serious novel, *Boy*, by the highly regarded author James Hanley, was published in London without much reaction, apart from favourable reviews. The book is a depressing study of a boy who runs away to sea, is sexually assaulted by members of the crew, contracts syphilis, and is eventually got rid of (drowned) by the captain to avoid a scandal! That summary is, of course, the sort of oversimplification that prompts some people to the wrong conclusion, yet no one could have accused Hanley of titillation (although among those who attacked the subject matter was Hugh Walpole who had rushed to the defence of *Jurgen*). Three impressions and many thousands of copies later, a cheap edition was issued in 1934, and a copy of that was seized from a public library. Objections were raised to its 'profane' language and in particular to a brothel scene, and the library as well as publisher were advised to plead guilty to obscene libel in January 1935, when the error of their ways was punished with a fine.

In the United States, 6000 copies of Wallace Smith's *Bessie Collier* (1935), the story of a Chicago prostitute, had been sold before exception was taken and fines levied. Something similar might have happened in England to another distinguished writer, Edward Carpenter, over his book *Love's Coming of Age*. The publisher Stanley Unwin, in his *The Truth About Publishing*, relates an incredible story about a visit from a detective asking that Carpenter's book be withdrawn. Mystified, Unwin pointed out that the book had been in print for *seven years* without complaint. When the nonplussed detective produced his marked copy, it transpired that every 'obscene' passage had been invested with a double meaning by the policeman. Fortunately, he was sensible enough to concede that his work had conditioned him into seeing obscenity where none existed.

7
'Modern' Erotica

The quotation marks on this chapter heading have been inserted because 'modern' in literary terms is almost impossible to define. In fiction, a writer's style may have little bearing on the age in which he lives; a number of popular present-day authors might be called 'old-fashioned', while others long since dead were well ahead of their time. Even my first example is something of a contradiction – a book published in 1977 of material written in the early 1940s – so the parameters for this chapter take in the past 50 years.

I have tried to limit the number of definitions of pornography, suggesting that one of the most reasonable is the 'deliberate attempt' to stimulate above all else. Yet even this guideline can be shot full of as many holes as there are talented writers trying their hands at the genre . . . which brings us back to my original contention – good writings as opposed to bad. Anaïs Nin (1904–77), mentioned almost incidentally earlier as the benefactress of Henry Miller when he was struggling for recognition, was also a gifted writer. The *New York Times Book Review* has called her 'one of the most extraordinary and unconventional writers of this century'.

A woman who never sought the limelight and who was apparently overshadowed for many years by the many talents around her, Anaïs Nin (her name reflects the mixed Spanish, Cuban, French and Danish ancestry) had her first book published in the 1930s. The quality of her writing was immediately apparent, yet the early works were either published privately or in small editions. It was not until the arrival of her autobiographical *Journals* in six volumes in the 1960s and 1970s, that the literary world at large rubbed the sleep from its eyes and hailed a 'new' genius. Among the many tributes paid to the *Journals* were: 'examines human personality with a depth and understanding seldom surpassed since Proust' (*Washington Post*), and 'a literary masterpiece, an illuminating social document' (London *Evening Standard*).

In case it should be thought I've been caught up in the cult hysteria surrounding Nin for the past twenty years, I'll balance the scales by pointing out that there is a school of thought that considers her overrated and that her tremendous intelligence and understanding of human nature come through in her writing more than any natural literary talent.

Nin's last book, *Delta of Venus*, published posthumously, is an anthology of erotica she wrote in the 1940s, when it was easier for penniless writers in Paris to earn money from porn than from 'legitimate' literature. She recalls that Henry Miller was offered $100 a month to write erotic stories, and her comment throws an interesting light on him: 'He rebelled because his mood of the moment was the opposite of Rabelaisian, because writing to order was a castrating occupation, because to be writing with a voyeur at the keyhole took all the spontaneity and pleasure out of his fanciful adventures.'

In an introduction to the collection Anaïs Nin wrote in 1976:

> At the time we were all writing erotica at a dollar a page, I realised that for centuries we had had only one model for this literary genre – the writing of men. I was already conscious of a difference between the masculine and feminine treatment of sexual experience. I knew there was a great disparity between Henry Miller's explicitness and my ambiguities – between his humorous, Rabelaisian view of sex and my poetic descriptions of sexual relationships in the unpublished portions of the diary . . . I had a feeling that Pandora's box contained the mysteries of woman's sensuality, so different from man's and for which man's language was inadequate. The language of sex had yet to be invented.

This assertion of a difference in *attitudes* is debatable. Margaret of Navarre (had she been born a few years later) might easily be compared with Rabelais, and D. H. Lawrence with Nin's 'poetic descriptions', although he would have been shocked at her subject matter. However, in purely physical terms – of 'specialist' knowledge – the differences can be used to advantage, such as this fairly typical passage from one of Nin's short stories:

> He crouched over so that he could take her with more force, touching the very bottom of her womb, touching the very flesh walls again and again, and then she experienced the sensation that within her womb some new cells awakened, new fingers, new mouths, that they responded to his entrance and joined in the rhythmic motion, that this suction was becoming gradually more and more pleasurable, as if the friction had aroused new layers of enjoyment. She moved quicker to bring the climax, and . . .

But irrespective of *whose* viewpoint (man or woman's) she adopts, her narrative style, her use of metaphor, is very effective, as this brief extract from the short story *Elena* reveals:

> When his fever rose, his breath was like that of some legendary bull galloping furiously to a delirious goring, a goring without pain, a goring which lifted her almost bodily from the bed, raised her sex in the air as if he would thrust right through her body and tear it, leaving her only when the wound was made, a wound of ecstasy and pleasure which rent her body like lightning, and let her fall again, moaning, a victim of too great a joy, a joy that was like a little death, a dazzling little death that no drug or alcohol could give but two bodies in love with each other, in love deep within their beings, with every atom and cell and nerve, and thought . . .

Since she was writing to order, at $1 a page, Anais Nin had to use her vivid imagination (although she suggests elsewhere that some of the 'team' would test and evaluate their ideas like cookery writers), and she leaves few situations unexplored, even sex with animals. But unlike the majority of truly pornographic material, Nin seldom repeats herself, and most of her writing is of a high standard. Take this fairly conventional lesbian scene:

> Silk again, silk under the fingers, silk between the legs, silky shoulders, neck, hair. Lips of silk trembling under the fingers. It was like the night at the opium den; the caresses lengthened, the suspense was preciously sustained. Each time they approached the orgasm, either Leila or Elena, observing the quickening of the motion, took up the kissing again – a bath of lovemaking, such as one might have in an endless dream, the moisture creating little sounds of rain between the kisses. Leila's finger was firm, commanding, like a penis: her tongue far-reaching, knowing so many nooks where it stirred the nerves.

> Instead of having one sexual core, Elena's body seemed to have a million sexual openings, equally sensitized, every cell of the skin magnified with the sensibility of a mouth. The very flesh of her arm suddenly opened and contracted with the passage of Leila's tongue or fingers. She moaned, and Leila bit into the flesh, as if to arouse a greater moan. Her tongue between Elena's legs was like a stabbing, agile and sharp. When the orgasm came, it was so vibrant that it shook their bodies from head to foot.

Even where she has to 'deliver the goods' and cut out the non-essential delicate touches, she manages to hold our attention. Our heroine Elena and her lesbian friend Leila are joined by a prostitute, Bijou:

> Under their feet was a big white fur. They fell on this, the three bodies in accord, moving against each other to feel breast against breast and belly against belly. They ceased to be three bodies. They became all mouths and fingers and tongues and senses. Their mouths sought another mouth, a nipple, a clitoris. They lay entangled, moving very slowly. They kissed until the kissing became a torture and the body grew restless. Their hands always found yielding flesh, an opening. The fur they lay on gave off an animal odor, which mingled with the odors of sex.
>
> Elena sought the fuller body of Bijou. Leila was more aggressive. She had Bijou lying on her side, with one leg thrown over Leila's shoulder, and she was kissing Bijou between the legs. Now and then Bijou jerked backwards, away from the stinging kisses and bites, the tongue that was as hard as a man's sex.
>
> When she moved thus, her buttocks were thrown fully against Elena's face. With her hands Elena had been enjoying the shape of them, and now she inserted her finger into the tight little aperture. There she could feel every contraction caused by Leila's kisses, as if she were touching the wall against which Leila moved her tongue. Bijou, withdrawing from the tongue that searched her, moved into a finger which gave her joy. Her pleasure was expressed in melodious ripples of her voice, and now and then, like a savage being taunted, she bared her teeth and tried to bite the one who was tantalizing her.
>
> When she was about to come and could no longer defend herself against her pleasure, Leila stopped kissing her, leaving Bijou halfway on the peak of an excruciating sensation, half-

crazed. Elena had stopped at the same moment.

Uncontrollable now, like some magnificent maniac, Bijou threw herself over Elena's body, parted her legs, placed herself between them, glued her sex to Elena's, and moved, moved with desperation. Like a man now, she thumped against Elena, to feel the two sexes meeting, soldering. Then as she felt her pleasure coming she stopped herself, to prolong it, fell backwards and opened her mouth to Leila's breast, to burning nipples that were seeking to be caressed.

Elena was now also in the frenzy before orgasm. She felt a hand under her, a hand she could rub against. She wanted to throw herself on this hand until it made her come, but she also wanted to prolong her pleasure. And she ceased moving. The hand pursued her. She stood up, and the hand again travelled towards her sex. Then she felt Bijou standing against her back, panting. She felt the pointed breasts, the brushing of Bijou's sexual hair against her buttocks. Bijou rubbed against her, and then slid up and down, slowly, knowing the friction would force Elena to turn so as to feel this on her breasts, sex and belly. Hands, hands everywhere at once. Leila's pointed nails buried in the softest part of Elena's shoulder, between her breast and underarm, hurting, a delicious pain, the tigress taking hold of her, mangling her. Elena's body so burning hot that she feared one more touch would set off the explosion. Leila sensed this, and they separated.

Another woman author, this time emerging from the pack of unknown writers thrown up by Olympia Press was Claire Rabe, although I must admit I don't know if that is her real name or one of the pseudonyms conceived by Girodias (*see* Chapter 10). There was an abundance of fresh and original talent in the Girodias stable, although much of the work from that series has a familiar ring about it, as though the young authors had not yet broken free of the umbilical cord. Ms Rabe's long short story *Sicily Enough* is in parts reminiscent of Henry Miller, although the heat of her Sicilian sun does seem to have a calming effect on the Miller-style of frenetic narrative. Here are a couple of illustrations:

Down below in Naxos, the first town built by the Greeks in Sicily, eating prehistoric octopus, while my eyes drift over the splendid view of my island above.

Worn, fabulous landslide of a view, green as black jagging to that sea where lava still lies exposed as it has lain for centuries.

Not thinking of the view; it has been sown into me. His body planted in me, I feel a tree. How shocking in the mirror, how very secret and deep it looks from the outside, while inside there is a wet intensity even deeper than what the mirror shows, and that's very deep. How cataclysmic to be penetrated, those thighs opening wide to let him in.

From a dusty fig tree I take a bursting fruit. It must be splitting to be good. As I am at my full opening, ripe and glad to have this pleasure made known to me. How many women are allowed this as they plough through years of intimacy that are never catastrophic. . . .

The sight of him wobbles my groin. Desire flares inside me as the sun on my back. Hot as hell and deep like that; red in all my corners, the thick smell of sex everywhere.

We make love like religion. He lets out my name with his sperm and I feel adored in a way that no virgin has ever been prayed to.

Lapped in waves of good feeling, free and solid my body rises for him. So profound is our contact, today I have forgotten my children. A holiday of the flesh, essential breathing flesh, connective tissue between day and night, before and after love, it's all a rhythm going towards and coming away from actual love which is intercourse.

That in me which can be touched responds only to him. My response is sudden gushes, my inside mucous flesh seems to detach itself from tough walls in an unbelievably painless wave. His very fingerprint is a profound mark on me. Like patterns in the desert that are, after all, the only sign of anything there, it doesn't matter how lasting. If the wind did not stir the sand the desert would have no movement at all.

Thus I lie under this hot Sicilian sun, sweating at last, waiting for more swells and rills.

Another interesting writer from the same stable was James Sherwood, whose novel *Stradella* also owed something to Henry Miller, although to give him credit much of the book, particularly his humour, is highly original. Even the more 'familiar' passages are strangely erotic:

I was enveloped in her. Every limb was burning. Every breath was searing. I was pinned to the bed by her onrush. My soldier rose like the sphinx, serenely taking its time.

She folded her arms around me. She lay on her back and buried my head in her breasts. Tentatively I kissed her nipples, a weightless fly flitting over her. They hardened and expanded, a ripe fruit unpeeled in her bed and laid bare. She plucked me like a dandelion. I sank my toe in her apple. She spread me over the sides of the bed, and sat herself down on me, a sea wave, corking breath. She moaned into the cushions. I held her above me, speared on my thumb, and spun her. She clutched blindly at my stem like a lariat and whirled me. Every place that I touched on her skin broke out like a wound, ripe and rosy. The tongue in my head, not a word on it, tilled her furrows and curves. She became a ripe pasture. The wounds broke out in blossoms. The curves turned to creeks of sweat. Her whole body ran like ore, a mother lode of golden bronze tan. . . .

. . . There really was a heaven and we knew, in those glances, where paradise was and how to find it on the map. We'd found it in the dark, and for us there was no doubt.

I threw her against a wall. She stuffed me in a drawer. She sighed and swung from a lamp. I crawled up the Venetian blinds. She whimpered and fell off the bed and split in 69 slivers. I pieced them together 9 times by 7 and had 6 left over which I ate. She wiped her lips with a spoonful of ice cream. I polished her toenails with ear wax. She made rings with her locks and a collar of braid. Our heads bumped in a pillowcase, condemned Siamese twins, and we waltzed over the upholstery, jigsaw puppets. She became the wall clock and I the hands. I wound up her back and she chimed the beats by seconds. She had the pendulum and I had the weights.

However, when our hero's love-making comes down to earth, Sherwood doesn't let him take anything for granted, and the ensuing scene conveys the frustrations of a love-match that was certainly not made in Heaven. The dialogue is bizarre yet uncomfortably true to life:

'Not this time.' Her commands issued forth without the bulb. My jaws ached.

'Not there . . . up a little . . . that's the spot . . . now easy . . . no, lower! Lower! O! O!' She made some joy sounds, then cursed. 'I don't know what's wrong! You hit the spot every night and morning last week! Now you can't seem to find it at all!'

'But maybe it's just not there anymore.'

> 'No, it is! It is! You don't know where to try.'
> 'But I am trying. I did try. The spot's moved. Here let me try again. My jowls are throbbing Stell – Stradella. I can't find it. I can't!'
> 'No it hasn't moved! It hasn't! It's still there! You don't know where to look. Keep trying. Keep looking.'
> 'Maybe if we turn the light on –'
> Eventually the cannon fired and the fodder plopped out of the barrel. As for me, I was a machine gun. Stroke one, stroke two, ratatatat.

The hero's mother is worthy of a character from a Tom Sharpe novel (*see* Chapter 8), and Sherwood's portrait is very vivid:

> 'Baby! What have you been doing? You haven't been home all week!' cried mother when I wandered into her bedroom. She was reclining.
> 'I've been –' I yelled and, grasping the air, swept on in proud triumph: 'Sleeping with – Queen of Rutland!'
> Mother set her vibrator aside. She'd shouted at me and I'd shouted in return because of the vibrator's noise. She fixed upon me her double-edged expression of long-suffering motherhood. It was supposed to be eternal and enduring and infinitely sublime. But she was finding it difficult to keep from breaking out laughing. The result was a smirk, and a fart.
> 'Baby – (pronounced: Baaaabbbyyy).' She drew out the syllables, increasing their scorn, evolving a sermon of Thou Shalt Not's. At the same time she was pulling the bed jacket around her so as not to reveal her all-too apparent breasts, thus embellishing the impression with some dignity. 'You – haven't been seeing a – tramp –'
> 'No mother. Of course not. But I'm going to dress up now.' I turned and went to my bedroom.
> 'Baby!' Wait!' Mother struggled out of the sheets and blankets, pulled off a piece of scotch tape that normally slept on her forehead all night to ward away advancing wrinkles. 'Baby! Come here and speak to your mother properly!'
> I was already down the hall at the other end of the house. Mother, with her bed jacket open and her transparent nightie spotted with spaghetti and oatmeal, marched into my bedroom barefooted, put her hands on her hips and stood in the doorway.

Literary reviews usually mean little to an author; he needs them but he realises, having swallowed his pride, that even a bad one can be as rewarding in promoting sales as a 'rave'. The most satisfying tribute of all is from the fellow writer whose own work he respects. In the 1950s, H. L. Humes earned the praise not only of the critics for his novel *The Underground City*, but that of distinguished writers such as Storm Jameson (one of the few great novels of our time) and Sir Noel Coward, who took the trouble to write a 'fan' letter. On the strength of this I read Humes' next novel *Men Die*, which turned out to be equally impressive in another way, but was also coincidentally highly erotic in places.

The story concerns Vanessa Hake, a wife of a navy commander who is killed in an explosion on a US navy base in the Caribbean just before World War II. One of the central characters is a young lieutenant, Everett Sulgrave, with whom the widow has an affair. One of the most impressive passages in the book is the following reflective daydream, in which Vanessa reviews with her alter-ego the events that lead to her present despair. Humes lets her tell the story, interrupting the long reminiscences only once with a short but searingly vivid piece of descriptive narrative:

funeral
his deathday party
thirty minutes I go downstairs still alive
I am still alive I am
Vanessa Lee Lynch Hake 38 lying abed naked
could have been a better wife to him *true or false*
Staring at ceiling
Unfamiliar ciel
bleu egg and dart Egganddart Hotel *true*
won't listen to this won't listen *yes true*
could have been a better husband damn his lovely
I am *He's gone*
Beautiful they tell me stunning they tell me
oh his baroness *really really gone*
movie star he told me he told me
Now he's gone *really really really gone*
dead they tell me oh
damn him damn him oh damn him damn
damn his dead eyes *poor lovely dead eyes* *love*

him *oh him him him him him*
Rollover smell of hotel sheets soothing and
smoothing tears stick starched sheets and
clean pillow pillows two pillows
one for my *belly one* for my head none for the
little boy who killed himself dead *gone*
gone gone gone

get used to he's gone
in thirty minutes I go downstairs
dirty ugly word funeral *body body who*
delivery of the body who will arrange
in transit *in delivery*
sic transit Call my young man
all staff and no rod to comfort me
ten hours bearing down

There is a disconnected scene which also haunts her, minor-keyed, evoked by memory of other funerals: remembered fragments float into mind; of being thrashed by her husband with a razor strop; and of her father, the old dead Admiral, who beat her once for wearing lipstick, at sixteen, a week after her mother's funeral. Sharp memories. In fury and in guilt and in helplessness, she rises naked from the bed and goes to the door. Lock it. Returns to bed, a secret person, and cries. Alone, full of love, she lies on her back, one pillow over her eyes, and locks her pillowed wrists between her legs. Rigid as lonely death, she re-enacts the furious scene, the shattering erotic dream, piecing together memories in her shuttered mind like shards of a smashed mirror. Lost in the lonely cycle of that mystery and that longing, she imagines now the conjunctions of carnal love, the entrances and withdrawals – still lying perfectly still, lost from time – arches her back for several minutes, neck rigid, teeth gritted, eyes blind with tears; is slowly trapped in rhythms of love experienced, in grinding memories of vanished flesh: nearly faints with the animal force of the final illumination.

It has been said that there are few truly original plots in fiction, most novels being a development of two or three basic storylines within a study of human relationships, especially the influence people have over each other. The author who introduces sexual relationships for example tends to be fascinated by the premise of man controlling woman, or woman manipulating man; but the subjugation of the will by an *outside*, totally dispassionate force is much more unusual. This is the theme of Luke Rhinehart's *The Dice Man*, mentioned in the Preface. Luke, the central character, is a disillusioned psychiatrist who has tried every known philosophy and religion and found them all wanting. But his life changes dramatically when he discovers a new Deity, the dice . . . sorry, Dice.

The attraction to Luke is that the dice offers a real alternative to the patterned order of society, substituting an entirely random behaviour pattern for what is to him the mind-blowing boredom of life's conventions and routines. The philosophy is to be free of constraints by living according to the 'wild' instructions of the dice. In ludo, for example, we unhesitatingly accept the dice's orders to move X places on the board. In *The Dice Man* Luke provides himself with a list of options for every decision – from one to six – and merely follows the option selected by the dice. No decision in business or private life is made without consulting the dice. At one stage it tells Luke at a cocktail party to alter his personality every five minutes, presenting himself with roles that are alien to the real Luke, roles that include that of the drooling idiot and the sex maniac (with painful results).

In the following scene, his new religion carried over into his work, Luke has decided to dispense with the traditional 'sounding board' role of the psychiatrist, and react in the way an ordinary person might react to another person's cry for help. But although to this patient, that 'normal' reaction means sex, Luke still remains professionally detached:

> As long as she had been my patient, however, I had not responded to her sexually one millimeter, or to any other female patient in five years, despite writhings, declarations, propositions, strippings and attempted rapes – all of which had occurred during one session or another. But the doctor-patient relationship froze my sexual awareness as completely as doing fifty push-ups under a cold shower. Looking at Linda Reichman smile and perceptibly arch her back and project her (true or false) bosom, I felt my loins, for the first time in my analytic history respond . . .
>
> 'I think maybe it would be good for both of us – if we got to know each other physically. Don't you?'
>
> She came to the chair and let her skirt fall to the floor. Her half-

slip must have gone with it. She had on white silk bikini-panties but no stockings. Sitting down in my lap (the chair tipped back another three inches with an undignified squeak), her eyes half-closed, she looked up into my face and said drowsily, 'Don't you?'

Frankly, the answer was yes. I had a fine erection, my pulse was forty percent, my loins were being activated by all the requisite hormones and my mind, as nature intended it in such cases, was functioning vaguely and without energy. Her lips and tongue came wetly against and into my mouth, her fingers along my neck and into my hair. She was role-playing Brigitte Bardot and I was responding accordingly. After a prolonged, satisfactory kiss, she stood up, and with a set, drowsy, mechanical half-smile removed, item by item, her blouse, bra (she hadn't needed falsies), bracelet, wristwatch and panties.

Since I continued to sit with a blissfully unplanned and idiotic expression she hesitated, and sensed that somewhere now was my cue to embrace her passionately, carry her to the couch and consummate our union. I decided to miss the cue. After this brief hesitation (her now wet upper lip twitched once), she knelt down beside me and fingered my fly. She undid the belt, a hook and lowered the zipper. Since I didn't move one millimeter (voluntarily) she had trouble extricating her desired object from my boxer undershorts. When she had succeeded in freeing him from his cage, he stood with dignified stiffness, trembling slightly, like a young scholar about to have a doctoral hood lowered over his head. (The rest of me was cold and immobile as the code of ethics of the AAPP encourages us.) She leaned forward to put her mouth over it.

'Did you ever see the movie, The Treasure of Sierra Madre?' I asked.

She stopped, startled, then closing her eyes completely, drew my penis into her mouth.

She did what intelligent women do in such cases. Although the warmth of her mouth and the pressure of her tongue produced predictable feelings of euphoria, I found I was not much mentally excited by what was happening. That mad scientist dice man was looking at everything too hard.

After what began to seem like an embarrassingly long time (I sat mute, dignified, professional through it all), she rose up and whispered. 'Take off your clothes and come.' She moved nicely to the couch and lay down on her stomach with her face to the wall.

I felt that if I sat immobile any longer she would snap out of it and become angry, get dressed and demand her money back. I had seen her in two roles, sex kitten and intellectual bitch. Was there some sort of third Linda? I walked over (my left hand pants clutching) to the couch and sat down. Linda's white, nude body looked cold and babyish against the formal brown leather. Her face was turned away but my weight on the side of the couch let her know I had arrived.

Whatever limitations Linda might have as a human being seemed adequately compensated for by a round and apparently firm posterior. Her instinct – or probably her well-learned habit – of stuffing her buttocks at an obviously aroused man seemed correct. My hand actually arrived within two and one-quarter inches of that flesh before the mad scientist in the London fog got the message through.

'Roll over,' I said. (Get her best weapon aimed elsewhere.)

She rolled slowly over, reached up two white arms and pulled my neck down until our mouths met. She began to groan authoritatively. She pressed first her mouth hard against mine and then, somehow getting me to lift my legs up on the couch beside hers, pressed her abdomen hard into mine. She tongued, writhed, groaned and clutched with intelligent abandon. I just lay, wondering not too acutely what to do.

Apparently I had missed another cue, because she broke our kiss and pushed me slightly away. For an instant I thought she might be abandoning her role, but her half-closed eyes and twisted mouth told me otherwise. She had parted her legs and was reaching for potential posterity.

'Linda,' I said quietly. (No nonsense about movies this time.) 'Linda,' I said again. One of her hands was playing Virgil to my Dante and trying to lead him into the underworld, but I held Dante back.

The concept of a dice-god may be pretty way out, but at least it has a strange simplicity – and certainly greater honesty than some of the Jesus freaks and messiahs that pop up from time to time, which was the subject of one of Leslie Thomas's lesser known novels, *The Man With the Power.* Leslie Thomas, in common with other prolific writers, is usually identified with one title, *The Virgin Soldiers* and is given little credit for his versatility and a professionalism that enables succeeding novels to retain a freshness not often found among bestsellers. Whether he is writing about sex in the suburbs, old folks turning to crime or the adventures of a sea captain, he introduces humour effortlessly, without disturbing the flow of the storyline. In *The Man With the Power* the hero's wife, a dancer, has left him and he goes to America to find her. He is caught up with a travelling troupe of conmen selling 'the word', and goes to bed with the nubile young daughter of their leader:

> . . . she was holding back the bedclothes for me to climb in and the white body was lying sheathed there. I went in beside her. She was like a warm lozenge. We embraced softly at first and then in earnest, almost crushing each other, my thin bones against her comfortable podginess. Her hands went to my thing.
>
> 'I bet you don't know what that is,' I said. . . .
>
> 'Let's try,' I said ambiguously. I eased her legs apart and began. It was very simple. We slid together easily, bringing a sweet gasp from her and a sharp memory suddenly returned for me. Sex is like taste, for me; I can never remember precisely what it's like until the next time. . . .
>
> Some women are thin screws, some are loose screws, some tight, some expansive. I've known women who needed a whole bedroom to perform, bed, floor, wall, dressing-table, stool, washbasin, and windowsill. Others have been neat and compact, economical in every movement. There was a girl at BBC Television once who would have fucked comprehensively on a matchbox. But Ambrosia was the first I had ever known to do it *in absentia*. From the moment I began to move she simply was not there. Her body was doing all the things, indeed half a dozen at the same time, but emotionally she had gone, departed. I leaned up on my hands and wrists and looked down at her. Her eyes were screwed up, like they were that solitary night of hers in Bethlehem, and her face was shut. Her body was moving rapidly, with mine, and those big breasts, dodging from side to side now seemed to be following me around. Then I realized that she had taken herself back to that room in Bethlehem, and a hundred lone rooms before that, and was doing it herself. I was merely a substitute for masturbation! She had, as they say in America, a lot of things going for her. But I wasn't one of them.
>
> Her climax was volcanic while I came only as a sort of courtesy. We lay quietly, sweating, after that and I retreated down her body and the bed until I was curled up in the vicinity of her

accommodating stomach. I felt her wake and she looked at me over the top of her breasts with an expression that said, for sure, 'Are you still here.'

'Lovely,' she whispered. 'Really lovely, Willy. I feel so satisfied.'

'You may be more than satisfied,' I said from my place against her belly. 'You may be pregnant.'

'Ah,' she said, still softly. 'Having a little worry down there are we? That's betting after the race, Willy.'

Using the simile or metaphor can be an economic yet doubly effective means of description. I'll never forget one of Raymond Chandler's heroes gazing at a sexy 'dame' and reflecting 'I was as randy as a stallion', conveying more in two words than some writers could in a page. Leslie Thomas paints as vivid a picture in the following scene in which the young lady just encountered is masturbating in front of our hero, and he offers to lend a hand.

Her warm, wet fingers guided mine to the place and I carried on where she had left off. I had never done that before. It was quietly exciting and selfishly unselfish, giving a nice feeling of sacrifice. I really enjoyed doing it and watching the brightening expression on her young face. 'Quicker, quicker now,' she asked me at the end, and I did. The effect was amazing. We had a second-hand washing machine once that used to leap up and down on its base when it was spin-drying and this is how Ambrosia went. She lay there panting her life away when it was done while I lay and smiled at her. She recovered sufficiently to kiss me.

In due course, Willy catches up with his wife. They go to bed for old times' sake:

We remained apart for a moment and then turned inwards and clutched at each other as though we had been lost and had been found again. I had forgotten how small her face was. My hands held it and my face pressed against it. I felt her tears on my cheek. 'Don't cry,' I said.

'No, I mustn't, must I,' she sniffed. 'There's nothing to cry about, is there? Nothing much, anyway. Why don't you take your pants . . . trousers off?'

'You do it,' I said against her face. 'See if you can remember.'

'I hear the zip has replaced the fly-button,' she giggled sadly.

'You can't stop progress,' I said.

Her fingers alighted on me, fumbling for the ear of the zip. She remained very close to me, burrowing into me as if she were afraid of something outside. She unzipped me firmly and slid both her hands into the aperture, cool, sweet fingers that touched my rearing flesh. . . .

Even a mild obsession with parts of the human anatomy is handled with originality.

'A blanket covers a multitude of sins,' she said. 'Your thing *is* rather noble, you know.' She poked her head inquisitively beneath the bedcovers. 'God,' she exclaimed. 'It is too. It's standing up like Nelson, looking at me with his one eye.'

'Very historic,' I said. 'Mind you I always did think that, for a cock, he is rather aristocratic.'

Silvie had many good parts, but her breasts were best of all. Now, exposed, they seemed to blink with surprise like small animals disturbed from sleep. They always brought out the hungry man in me and to see them again was to see a lost delicacy. But I kissed her mouth just to show I was not greedy. My God, I thought, how I am going to enjoy her.

'Wake up,' I said, kissing one nipple. Then: 'Rise and shine,' kissing the other.

'They get lazy,' she murmured. 'When they're not working. I have to give them a brisk slap sometimes before I go on-stage. Some of the girls do it to each other, but I haven't got that far yet.'

Sometimes I used to think her back was better than her front, although I could never really make up my mind.

I laid my head like a dog, sideways across her shoulder blades, enjoying the sensation of the superb skin against my face. How careless I had been to allow her to go. Her backbone was white and curved beautifully, like the seam in a long piece of celery. I put my cheek to her cheeks. 'I think your arse has got a bit bigger,' I said.

'Oh, no!' Her jerk threw my head sideways. 'Oh, don't say that, Willy.' She saw my face in the dim light and saw that I was grinning. 'Oh, you are a rotten swine,' she said, but with relief. 'You know how I worry like mad about that.'

'Your arse is like it always was,' I said, kissing her mouth and eyes. 'Like a tulip.'

'What colour?'

'A white one. White as ice-cream.'

And finally, after the survey of parts, the union is consummated:

> 'That's good. Willy, I want you so much. I want you inside me. Can we put anything else off for a bit and do it now?'
>
> I turned her with one hand and felt her knees draw up either side of my waist. I was crouching in front of her, our eyes fixed with bright animal excitement on each other's eyes. Her little, lovely hands went out underneath me, caught my stem and tugged me to her. We were both slippery with anticipation. I eased myself an inch at a time until her gentle legs had closed about me like a trap. Then our parts touched with a soft shock. I swear we were not joined by more than a quarter of an inch. Her mouth opened and her face creased, becoming strangely old in the half-light. I watched her closely, then pushed myself into her and watched her sweet face clear. We were man and wife again. Briefly. . . .'

Returning to the point I made in the previous chapter about sado-masochism, *The Story of O* by Pauline Réage (a pseudonym), first published in France in 1954 and considered too pornographic for the English language for almost ten years, is a book which has as its *raison d' être* the enslavement of the mind by force. What keeps *The Story of O* above the level of porn – and highly erotic even to those who find the subject distasteful – is the author's exploration of the mind and motivation of his central character. Written in a style that is simple, direct and frighteningly vivid, the plot is concerned with the subjugation of O's will, a will that is in any case 'betrayed' by desires locked in her subconscious. On the surface, typical of the books to which many women object, the story is, admittedly, concerned with the exploitation and degradation of women, and while I cannot claim that the sex is incidental, the book is principally about love and humility, and *might* have worked even if the sexes had been reversed.

The central character, O, is taken by her lover to a mysterious house in a suburb of Paris, where she is left without explanation in the care of a form of secret society dedicated to the 'pleasures' of sado-masochism. Her role is explained by one of her new masters:

If our night-time costume, what we are wearing now, leaves our sex uncovered, it is not for the sake of convenience, since it would be just as convenient otherwise, but for that of insolence, so that your eyes will focus themselves there and nowhere else, so that you will come finally to understand that there resides your master, your lord, to whom all of you is destined and above all your lips. In the day, when we are dressed in the usual manner and you as you are now, you will observe the same rule and when requested you will simply open our clothing and later close it again when we are finished with you. Also, at night, you will have only your lips wherewith to do us honour, and also your widespread thighs, since, at night, you will have your hands secured behind your back and you will be nude, as you were when brought here a short while ago; you will not be blindfolded save when you are to be maltreated and, now that you have seen yourself being beaten, when you are whipped. In this regard, if it were advisable that you accustom yourself to whipping – and it shall be frequent, daily, so long as you remain here – it is *less for our pleasure than for your instruction* [my italics, RHL]. This may be stressed by the fact that, on those nights when no one wants you, you may expect a visit from the valet who has been appointed to the job: he will enter your cell and, in the solitude, mete out to you what you need to receive and which we are not inclined to bestow. Actually, the object of these procedures, as well as of the chain which will be affixed to your collar, is to confine you to within a limited scope and more or less to your bed for several hours every day, a good deal less to make you suffer pain, scream or shed tears than, by means of this pain, to enforce upon you the idea that you are subject to constraint and to teach you that you utterly belong to something which is apart from and outside yourself.

Because of the great depths of her love, O agrees unquestioningly to stay at the house, where she is treated as a slave, subjected to violence of every sort, including regular beatings and sexual abuses of the most debasing kind by men she is not allowed to see, or even look at, so submissive is her role. On the first night, after savage assaults of both kinds, O is taken to a cell and left chained to her bed. Despite the trauma and disorientation she has experienced, O's initial thoughts are revealing:

Lying on her left side, and alone in the darkness and the silence,

> hot between the two layers of fur, O wondered why such a great mildness mingled with the terror within her, or why terror should have such a sweet taste. She became aware that, in large measure, her distress was caused by her inability to use her hands; not that her hands could have protected her (did she indeed really desire to protect herself?), but, her hands free, she would have been able to make a gesture of self-defense, a little gesture, would have made a little attempt to thrust away the hands that had seized her, the flesh that had transpierced her, to shield her flesh from the whip. They had sundered her from hands, freed her of them; her body under the fur, her own body itself was inaccessible to her; how odd it was, not to be able to touch one's own knees, nor the slit of one's own womb. Her lips, the lips between her own legs, which were burning her, were forbidden to her, and perhaps burned her because she knew they were open, awaiting whoever might happen to want them: openly awaiting Pierre, the valet, if he were to choose to enter between them. She was amazed to find that the memory of the whip could leave her so tranquil, so serene; whilst the thought that she would probably never know which of the four men had twice forced himself into her behind, nor know if it had indeed been man who had done it two times, nor know whether it might not have been her lover – this thought overwhelmed her. She slithered up and down on her belly for a moment, thinking that her lover loved the furrow between her buttocks, that he had never before this evening (if it had been he) penetrated her there.

O's weak lover, René, tries, somewhat belatedly, to give her moral support through the remainder of the initiation period, and before leaving her 'unprotected', gives the first partial explanation for his strange behaviour:

> He told her that she belonged and was ultimately answerable to him, only to him, even if she were to receive orders from others than he, no matter whether he were there or absent, for by way of principle he concurred in no matter what she might be required to do or might be inflicted upon her; and that it was he who possessed and enjoyed her through the agency of those into whose hands he surrendered her, and this was so from the mere fact that she was surrendered to them by him, she was the gift, he the donor. She was to show obedience to them all, and greet them with the same respectfulness she greeted him, as so many images of him. Thus

> would he possess her as a god possessed his creatures whereupon he lays hands guised as some monster or bird, as some invisible spirit or as ecstasy itself. He did not want to, he was not going to leave her. The more he subjected her to, the more important to him she would become. The fact he gave her to others was proof thereof, proof in his eyes, it ought to be proof also in hers, that she belonged to him. He gave her so as to have her immediately back, and recovered her enriched a hundredfold in his eyes, as is an ordinary object that has served some divine purpose and thereby become infused with sanctity. For a long time he had desired to prostitute her, and it was gladly he now discovered that the pleasure he reaped from it was greater than he had even dared hope, and increased his attachment to her as it did hers to him, and that attachment would be the greater, the more her prostitution would humiliate and soil and ruin her. Since she loved him, she had no choice but to love the treatment she got from him. O listened and trembled from happiness; since he loved her, she trembled, consentingly.

In his absence, O is subjected to complete sexual humiliation yet, almost like the religious martyrs of a past age, she seems now to have acquired an inner serenity:

> A hideous satiety of pain and joy ought, one would have thought, to have edged her further and further along that gradually declining slope at whose lower depths are sleep and somnambulism. But to the contrary. The corset which held her upright, the chains which maintained her in subjection, silence, her sanctuary – perhaps these had something to do with it, as may have had the constant spectacle of girls being pressed to use, and even when they were not undergoing use, the spectacle of their at all times accessible bodies. The spectacle also and the awareness of her own body. Daily and, as it were, ritualistically soiled by saliva and sperm, by sweat mingled with her own sweat, she sensed herself to be, literally, the vessel of impurity, the gutter whereof Scripture makes mention. And yet in all, those parts of her body which were the most continually offended, having become more sensitive, seemed to her to have become, at the same time, more lovely, and as though ennobled: her mouth clamped upon anonymous members, the points of her breasts hands forever were fondling, and between her wideflung thighs, the twin ways leading into her

belly, avenues trod by a whole wide world to pleasure. However astonishing it were, that from being prostituted her dignity might increase, the crucial point was nonetheless one of dignity. It illuminated her as if from within, and one could see her calmness in her bearing, upon her countenance the serenity and imperceptible inner smile one rather guesses at than perceives in the eyes of the recluse.

The book is so sensitively handled by the author (the term 'genius' was used by more than one respected reviewer) that its publication was inevitable in an enlightened society, whether one considers it pornographic or not – Graham Greene is one who hedged his bets, saying that it was, but describing it as 'well written and without a trace of obscenity'. Significantly the film version – by the man who directed *Emmanuelle*, one of the first soft-porn films to gain acceptance because of its chocolate-box beauty – has failed to get a certificate in English-speaking countries. That surely says much for the unique qualities of the written word. Literature provides fidelity and nuances of meaning that no other medium can match.

8
Humour in Erotica

Pornography is a serious business, whether you're writing, selling or reading the stuff. By its very nature, even conventional sex placed in a clandestine setting, puts on a solemn face. The concept of half-an-hour in bed or swinging from the chandelier with your favourite dream god/goddess, is a sobering thought in the cold light of day, enough to make the palms of your hands perspire. Indeed, this very earnestness is the only thing many of us find distasteful about pornography. We don't have pornographic dreams because we're invariably relaxed and in command of the situation (if it's a good dream). This is one of the basic differences between porn and erotica.

Moreover, because the subject is seldom funny, to accomplish the twin effects of exciting or stimulating the reader, as well as making him/her laugh, requires very special skills. With few exceptions humorous writers don't receive their due from the literary establishment – nor, for that matter, do most authors who choose to work in a narrow genre, science fiction or the world of the thriller, for instance – but those who can be funny when relating torrid sex scenes are an even rarer breed.

Many critics put Tom Sharpe (born 1928) in the same mould as Evelyn Waugh and P. G. Wodehouse, and his books are a most original blend of satire and farce. Perhaps I'm cheating slightly by starting with Sharpe because although sex plays an integral part in all of his stories, it is not likely to turn you on, unless you happen to share one of the fetishes with which his characters are currently preoccupied. However, since we're also dealing with kinky sex, Sharpe is relevant because his prose is brilliantly hilarious, but conceals a remarkably keen insight into behaviour patterns in society. His first two books, *Riotous Assembly* and *Indecent Exposure* are savage satires on the whites of South Africa, from where he was deported in 1961, after a ten-year residence. Both books follow the fortunes of the same key characters, stalwarts in the South African police, concerned with protecting their Shangri-La from the blacks – and the English, who in Sharpe's world are no less ludicrous.

Other writers have come up with a funny idea and developed it, but all Sharpe's well-plotted stories have a succession of different situations, each more bizarre and funny than the last. I wouldn't want to dismiss the 'one idea' category, but they seldom make great demands on an author's inventiveness. *Les Bijoux Indiscrets* (1747), by the French philosopher and writer Denis Diderot (1713–84) is fairly typical: the story of a prince who obtains a magic ring which makes a woman's vagina talk like a mouth, revealing the most intimate secrets of what it had been doing. The concept is quite original, but the 'gossip' less so.

Talking vaginas may smack of fantasy yet the concept is no more startling than the variety of sexual perversions indulged in by Sharpe's crazy but very real people.

In *Indecent Exposure*, Kommandant van Heerden and his colleagues take practical measures to combat the danger of 'interracial sex' between his white police and black women. Treatment takes the form of aversion shock therapy, erotic pictures of black women accompanied by electric shocks to the genitals, but, naturally, in a Sharpe novel, the plan misfires.

In *Porterhouse Blue*, Sharpe's first novel set in England, in fact at Cambridge where he was educated and where he subsequently lectured, the power politics of university life are vividly recreated. The writing is *so* clever that one tends to admire and envy Sharpe's style rather than laugh spontaneously, but one scene in which a totally ineffectual student tries to get rid of unwanted contraceptives is one of the funniest passages I have ever read. It has an air of realistic fantasy that reminds me of Stephen Leacock at his best, except, of course, that the subject matter is slightly different! The student, Zipser, decides the time has come to lose his virginity to the lecherous cleaning woman, Mrs Biggs, as overwhelmingly obese as Miss Hazelstone (of *Riotous Assembly*) is emaciated. Unable to face the ordeal of buying contraceptives in the normal way, he manages, through a chapter of disasters, to end up with a wholesale supply. They cannot be concealed in his room so he has to get rid of them.

His first thought was to flush them down the lavatory but the resourceful contraceptives won't be 'put down' and continue to resist Zipser's efforts. However, desperation lends ingenuity and his belated solution is to blow them up like balloons with carbon monoxide from the gas tap and release them through the chimney. The sky above the college is soon filled with strange looking floating objects, but snow icing up the chimney exit causes a bottleneck.

Alas, predictably, poor Zipser's subterfuge was in vain. The whole world was to learn about his liaison with Mrs Biggs, after that good lady had joined him in bed next morning, pausing only to light the gas fire!

In *Blott on the Landscape*, which deals with skulduggerous efforts to drive a giant motorway through a stately home and the efforts of the gardener, Blott, to forestall the forces of evil, Sharpe's principal sex athlete is another monstrosity. Lady Maud Lynchwood is not only monumentally unattractive but, as part of the landed aristocracy, she is barely aware of Blott's love and devotion. In due course this unlikely siren attempts to seduce the man from the Ministry whose help she needs in resisting the motorway, but he flees in terror.

Lest it be assumed that Sharpe has a down on the female sex, I should point out that Lady Maud is basically a sympathetic character; the villain of the piece is her husband, Sir Giles, who, naturally, has more than his share of unnatural practices. Sir Giles is into bondage – being tied up in baby clothes by Nanny Whip!

Most of Sharpe's heroes are adrift on an ocean of troubles, disorientated and in any case inadequate to the issues. In *Wilt*, lecturer Henry Wilt, always out of depth in trying to cope with indifferent adult students and an even more indifferent wife Eva (another gargantuan female) finds sex a little daunting.

At a party for her 'swinging' friends Sally, a sexual athlete friend of Eva, tries to seduce Wilt, who is barely able to cope with his wife's demands, let alone an unwanted mistress, and he repels her advances. But she takes her revenge, which is not difficult since Wilt is a walking disaster area, on this occasion walking into a cupboard and knocking himself out. He recovers to find himself 'impaled' on a life-size plastic doll, designed for a specific purpose. His attempts to escape culminate in him falling off the lavatory seat and getting knocked out again.

The perils of standing on a toilet seat, whether cohabiting with a plastic doll or the real thing, are spelt out in another novel, which just goes to show it can't be as uncommon as you thought! *Candy* by Terry Southern and Mason Hoffenberg, a very different book from *Wilt*, has enjoyed a far wider audience. It caused a sensation in the United States when it was first published in 1964, subsequently managing to maintain that interest in the best possible way – sales to date are well over six million copies.

Candy Christian is a beautiful young innocent who takes pity on those (males) in need. Unable to say 'no' to anyone, she reminds me of an emancipated Justine, except that this young lady doesn't exactly *suffer* the consequences. The novel satirises sexual attitudes in American society, and its literary value lies more in its originality than what passes for a plot, which is merely a development of one situation repeated in different guises. These cover Candy's sexual escapades with a Mexican gardener, professor, doctor, mystic and sundry others including her uncle. It is a highly professional 'manufactured' novel more than a work of brilliance as some of the critics said at the time, although a couple of Candy's adventures are unquestionably hilarious.

The toilet seat incident occurs when a panting doctor persuades her that she needs a gynaecological check-up regularly . . . in fact now, *this minute*, in Manhattan's Riveriera bar:

> Candy was amazed. 'Here? In the Riviera? Good Grief, I don't . . .'
>
> 'Oh yes,' said Dr. Johns. 'Just here . . . this will do nicely.' He had led the girl to the door on the men's toilet, and quickly inside. It was extremely small, a simple cabinet with a stool, nothing more. He locked the door.
>
> 'Good Grief,' said Candy, 'I really don't think . . .'
>
> 'Oh yes,' Dr. Johns assured her, 'perfectly all right.' He put his little bag down and started taking off her skirt. 'Now we'll just slip out of these things,' he said.
>
> 'Well, are you sure that . . .' Candy was quite confused.
>
> 'Now, the little panties,' he said, pulling them down. 'Lovely things you wear,' he added and lifted her up onto the stool.
>
> 'Now you just stand with one foot on each side of the stool, limbs spread, that's right and . . . oh yes, you can brace yourself with your hands against the walls . . . yes, just so. . . . Fine!'
>
> He bent, clutching the precious girl to him with such force and

abandon that her feet slipped off the stool and into the well of it. During the tumult the flushing mechanism was set in motion and water now surged out over the two of them, flooding the tiny cabinet and sweeping out of it and into the bar.

There was a violent pounding at the door.

'What in God's name is going on in there?' demanded the manager, who had just arrived. He and the bartender were throwing their weight against the door of the cabinet which by now was two feet deep in water as the doctor and Candy thrashed about inside.

'Good Grief!' she kept saying. They had both fallen to the floor. The doctor was snorting and spouting water.

Finally with a great lunge the two men outside broke open the door. They were appalled by the scene.

'Good God! Good God!' they shouted. 'What in the name of God is going on here!'

A police officer arrived at that moment and was beside himself with rage at the spectacle.

The doctor had lost consciousness by the time he was pulled to his feet. Both he and Candy were sopping wet and completely dishevelled. She was naked from waist down.

'He's a doctor!' she cried to the policeman, who was dragging him about like a sack and pulling her by the arm.

'Uh-huh,' said the cynical cop, 'Dr Caligari, I suppose.'

At other times, Candy at least starts off in control of the situation, although the seeds of her ideas seldom bear fruit. Taking pity on her father's Mexican gardener whose knowledge of English seems to be limited to 'Whot?', she finally persuades him to come to her bedroom that night:

Promptly at midnight Emmanuel arrived, entering across the roof and through Candy's window as they had planned. Candy lay stretched on the bed, the veritable picture of provocation, her blond hair spread like golden flames across the silken rose-lit pillow, and the black shimmering nightgown clinging to her body which lay with a slight reptilian curve, lush at the breast and thigh, lithe and willowy along the waist and limbs.

The gardener stared in amazement; it was too much like a movie or a folktale for him to fully believe, as the lovely girl stretched out her arms, half closed-eyed, whispering:

'Darling, I knew you would come.'

He was dressed as he had been earlier in the day; and still wearing his sneakers, he made no noise as he crossed the carpeted floor to the bed and took the girl in his arms.

'Undress quickly, my darling.' Candy breathed, 'and don't make a sound.' She put a finger to her lips and made her eyes wide to emphasize the necessity of this.

Emmanuel was in the bed in a trice, embracing her feverishly, and snatching her gown at once up to her shoulders.

'Oh, you do need me so!' the closed-eyed girl murmured, as yet not feeling much of anything except the certainty of having to fit this abstraction to the case.

'Oh my baby, my baby,' she whispered. She closed her eyes again and called upon Professor Mephesto's words; 'The needs of man are so many . . . and so aching.' 'Oh how you ache for me, my darling!' She flung both arms around his neck, and the gardener would have entered her then, with a terrible thrust to the hilt, so to speak . . . had not a padded scurrying sounded at that moment in the hall.

'Good Grief,' said Candy, in a very odd voice, 'it's Daddy!' pushing her hands violently against the gardener's chest. 'It's Daddy!'

And true enough, the door burst open at that instant and Mr Christian appeared, looking like some kind of giant insane lobster-man. At the sight of them he reeled, his face going purple, then hatefully black, as he crashed sideways against the wall, smashed back by the sheer impact of the spectacle itself. It was not as though he couldn't believe his eyes, for it was a scene that had formed a part of many of his most lively and hideous dreams – dreams which began with Candy being ravished, though it was (in the finale) she who was the aggressor, she who was voraciously ravishing them. So that now, actually confronted by the scene, one would think he was not unprepared, yet as dreams of death do not prepare a young man for the firing squad, but perhaps only build to the terrible intensity of it, so Mr Christian appeared now to be actually strangling with shock.

'. . . urg . . . ack . . . chchch,' were the sounds he produced for the first moment as he clawed at the air in front of him; then he came toward them like a man on stilts, picking up a chair and raising it stiffly over his head.

'Daddy!' cried Candy, in real alarm, but it was too late, for he swung the chair down at Emmanuel, who was leaping from the bed; it missed him and shattered against the bedpost. But he still retained a leg of the chair, and this, as a club, was a more formidable weapon than the chair itself, as he came relentlessly forward after the gardener, managing at last to speak through his grating teeth:

'You . . . You . . . You . . . COMMUNIST!'

I picked up a copy of *Someone is Killing the Great Chefs of Europe*, by Nan and Ivan Lyons because I enjoy thrillers and exotic foods and, as the dust jacket blurb entreated, 'its well worth reading for the menus alone'. In fact, the title was already familiar because the film version had been well publicized as an exciting romp, although the critics were not convinced. However, the novel turned out to be better, and the authors' treatment of sex as well as food, shows the hallmark of the connoisseur. The title is self-explanatory. The American hero and heroine are Max Ogden, owner of a chain of convenience-food restaurants, and his beautiful ex-wife Natasha O'Brien, cook supreme and famous food columnist. Since Natasha is understandably less than turned on by omelettes, she consoles herself with a number of lovers with a greater appreciation of the best things in life. One of them is Louis Kohner, perhaps the greatest chef in Europe, who is later to be found baked to death in his hotel oven. Not, fortunately, before the lovers can compare notes on *haute cuisine* flavouring:

It was morning. Louis had sensed it even without opening his eyes. 'Tasha,' he murmured to reassure himself. He turned to lie on his stomach, careful to position himself so that his genitals rested on the open palm of her outstretched hand. He opened his eyes to find her mouth, and as they kissed, her fingers involuntarily tightened around the stiffening pressure on her palm. They kissed again, their eyes open.

'I do so love to be awakened by a cock growing,' she said.

'You're hurting,' he said, pulling back slightly, as she released her grip.

'I'm sorry, Liebchen,' She raised herself and bent forward to kiss his penis. Then she stretched out, her head resting on his leg as she began to lick and caress the wounded area. Louis arched his back and moved his head so that he pressed his nose between her legs. She felt his tongue start to search inside her.

'You know,' she said as she began licking the length of his penis, 'you could stand a little salt, darling.'

Louis raised his head, breathing hard. He used the back of his hand to wipe the moisture from his lips. 'Had the recipe been mine, I would have added tarragon.'

'Don't be ridiculous, love,' she said, catching her breath as she took the head of his penis from her mouth, 'you never knew the right use for tarragon.' She cupped her hands around his testicles. 'For example, that salad in Rouen . . .'

Louis narrowed his eyes while his fingers continued exploring deep inside her. 'And what was wrong with my salad in Rouen?'

'Oh,' she moaned in response to the strength in his hand. 'I told you, love, it was the tarragon that was all wrong.'

'It was superb . . .' He winced sharply. 'Don't bite,' he said. 'It was a superb salad.'

'No, darling,' she answered, breathing heavily, 'I'm sorry, but I didn't mean to bite that hard. The salad was a disaster. You just can't add tarragon to endive without making the endive schizophrenic. Oh, that's marvellous,' she whispered.

Louis was on top of her. Her arms closed tightly around him. He began to penetrate. Slowly, slowly, slowly as he asked her, 'And what did you think of my Pigeonneaux last night?'

Natasha pressed her fingers into his back. 'Ach, mein Führer, the only thing better than your cooking is your fucking.'

After another chef is found drowned in a restaurant's giant fish-tank, Natasha is questioned by an Italian police captain Gilli and ends up in bed with him. They are awakened by a phone call from her ex-husband Max:

'Hello?'

'Miss Natasha O'Brien, please. Paris is calling.'

Gilli stirred. 'For me?' he asked sleepily.

'No,' she said. 'Yes, operator. I am Natasha O'Brien.'

Gilli moved his hand under the sheet and began to caress her breast.

'Nat? Nat? It's me, Millie.'

'Millie? Did you hear?' she asked.

Gilli began to pinch her nipples. She traced the outline of his lips with her finger.

'The chef at the American Embassy called me. I couldn't believe it. Are you all right?'

Gilli put his mouth to her nipples and rubbed them with his tongue. Natasha breathed in sharply.

'Yes. I think so.'

'You sound terrible, Nat.' Gilli's hands were moving across her body. 'You must be going through hell,' Max said.

Natasha began to pinch Gilli's nipples. 'You wouldn't believe what I'm going through now,' she said. Gilli's hand pushed her legs apart. 'It's incredible.'

'Listen, Nat, you've got to get out of there. How much can you take?'

Natasha held Gilli's penis in her hand. 'I don't know. Not too much more.'

'Then for Chrissake get on the next plane, and meet me in Paris.'

Gilli was on top of her, entering with force. 'Oh,' she said.

'I know,' Max replied. 'It must be more than you can bear.'

'Oh, my God, yes. Yes.'

'Nat, it's breaking my heart to hear you this way.' Gilli was rocking rapidly. Natasha put her arm around his neck and held tightly to him. 'Nat, when can you get here?'

'I'll come as fast as I can,' she said, rocking with Gilli.

'Is that a promise?' Max asked. 'I want to be with you, Nat. I know how alone you must be. It must be so hard for you.'

'Yes,' she breathed into the receiver.

'Nat, you sound really bad. How soon can you come?'

'I'm coming,' she whispered.

'When?' Max asked.

'Now, now, right now, as I'm talking to you. Oh, Millie, it's unbelievable.'

'Nat, don't let yourself go like that. Please. Pull yourself together. Please. It'll be all right. I promise you.'

Gilli withdrew but remained on top of her.

'Where are you?' she asked.

'The Plaza. How soon can you leave?'

Natasha looked at Gilli. 'How soon can I leave?' she repeated. He shrugged his shoulders as he put his arms around her. 'I don't know,' she said. 'I'm being held by the police.' Gilli smiled.

Such sophistication and experience is breathtaking, worthy of a heroine from one of the great sex classics. Few of them stray off the main path of eroticism with an introduction of humour, but *The Golden Lotus* (*Chin P'ing Mei*), to which I referred earlier, was written for entertainment, and the author treats his characters light-heartedly, yet with affection. There are several passages which are downright funny, like this reflection on a woman's mentality, her sense of priorities, even in the throes of passion. The hero, Hsi-men, had an enthusiasm for artificial aids, in drug form or for external application, that would have rocketed sales at sex shops of the day. In the following incident, he has sustained himself with an opium pill before returning to his wife's service with renewed vigour. Then he 'put some red powder upon his member and inserted it once again; and seizing her firmly by the legs, he attacked her two or *three thousand times* [my italics]. Golden Lotus' eyes closed and she began to tremble. "Darling," she whispered, "don't thrust so roughly; you will make my hair untidy." '

Luke Rhinehart, the author mentioned in my preface and discussed in the previous chapter, seems to dispense with the convention of heroes and heroines in *The Dice Man*, although we react in much the same way to his major characters. Early in the story, Luke 'discovers' his new god and in his first experiment the dice orders him late one night, with his wife asleep, to go downstairs and rape his partner's wife:

> As I walked woodenly down the two flights of stairs I noticed rust spots on the railing and an abandoned advertising circular crumpled into a corner. 'Think Big,' it urged. On the Ecstein floor I wheeled like a puppet, marched to the door of their apartment and rang. My next clear thought swept with dignified panic through my mind: 'Does Arlene really take the pill?' A smile coloured my consciousness at the thought of Jack the Ripper, on his way to rape and strangle another woman, and worrying whether she was protected or not.
>
> After twenty seconds I rang again.
>
> A second smile (my face remained wooden) flowed through at the thought of someone else's already having discovered the die and thus now busily banging away at Arlene on the floor just on the other side of the door.
>
> The door unlatched and opened a crack.

'Jake?' a voice said sleepily.

'It's me, Arlene,' I said.

'What do you want?' The door stayed open only a crack.

'I've come downstairs to rape you,' I said.

'Oh,' she said, 'just a minute.'

She unlatched and opened the door. She was wearing an unattractive cotton bathrobe, possibly even Jake's, her black hair was straggling down her forehead, cold cream whitened her face, and she was squinting at me without her glasses like a blind beggar woman in a melodrama of the life of Christ.

Closing the door behind me I turned toward her and waited, wondering passively what I was going to do next.

In vivid contrast to Rhinehart's anarchistic, essentially modern style, Robert Nye's *Falstaff*, which won the *Guardian* fiction prize in 1976, purported to be a memoir of the fifteenth century which he had 'transcribed, arranged and edited in modern spelling'. How much of Sir John Falstaff's rumbustious reputation is based on fact is hard to say, but Nye completes the picture that history has acquired from Shakespeare. Following the same sequence of events, he achieves the almost-impossible, making Falstaff even more entertaining. We also learn more about his sexual prowess, although when the libertine eventually marries, the account of the nuptials after a frolic in the snow is provided by Mistress Quickly. Nye reports as follows:

Then Sir John plunged with his potency of snow!
Dame Milicent bucked.
Dame Milicent kicked.
Dame Milicent wrestled.
Dame Milicent rolled in the snow like a scalded cat.
But O now Sir John, he would give her no quarter.
But O now Sir John, he would show her no mercy.
He broached that proud Dame.
Sir John impaled Dame Milicent on his great icicle.
Sir John made love to his lady like an avalanche.
He had her.
He joyed her.
He manned her.
He managed her.
He picked her lock.
He pleased her, he ploughed her, and O how he possessed her.

He rammed her.
He rode her.
He scaled her.
He served her.
He stabbed her.
He stuffed her.
He foined her.
He tupped her.
She took him upwards and downwards and sideways and everyways.
She took him in her belly, and wagging her tail.
O Jesu, O my lord, but how he fucked her!
Fixed her and foxed her and fetched her and fexed her.
Figged her and firked her and ferred her and fired her.
Forked her, all frosty, and brought her to fruition.
Of function.
Of junction.
Of conversation, copulation, much ado, the taming of the shrew.
Of carnal stings and spendings and sweet spicery.
She was his Juliet. He her Romeo.
She was his Cressida. He her Troilus.
She was his Cleopatra. He her Antony, bestriding her
Like a Colossus.
And all was well that ended well.
And all this glory ended with an O,
Foaming.
Oes and eyes.
So deep an O.
So full an O.
So overflown, so fucked
an O. And O. And
O. An
o

Before leaving humour, I'm obliged to acknowledge the contribution made by the limerick, although the style is invariably vulgar as opposed to erotic. A large number relate stories about the sexual organs, and of every imaginable (and unimaginable) sexual practice. According to Gershon Legman, who edited perhaps the largest collection ever compiled, *The Limerick*, the mid-eighteenth century saw the limerick 'laundered out of existence'; fortunately, there have been periodic revivals. A more charming example from the above collection deals with the legendary lovers:

> 'For the tenth time, dull Daphnis,' said Chloe
> 'You've told me my bosom is snowy;
> You have made much fine verse on
> Each part of my person.
> Now *do* something – there's a good boy!'

Finally, another piece of 'fine verse' that I find charming has a contradictory quality about it. It strikes me as typically modern, and yet it was published nearly half a century ago; typically American, and yet I can't read it without thinking of Professor Higgins (at least, the *My Fair Lady* version). Called 'The Twin Buttes', it was written by Earl H. Emmons:

> I once was calm, reserved and shy,
> A rather quiet sort of guy,
> A simple scribe of artless odes and sonnets,
> But that's before I chanced to stray
> In that brassiere display
> Where lovely ladies modeled bosom bonnets.
>
> And now my simple lyric soul
> Is prone to rear and rip and roll;
> I'm frisky as a dozen playful kittens;
> And I'm afraid I'm not the same
> Since those divine upholstered dames
> Exhibited their mamillary mittens.
>
> Now I admit that here and there
> Among the sex described as fair
> I've looked at bosoms foreign and domestic
> From puny papillary warts
> And sagging saddle-baggy sorts,
> To massive mounds impressive and majestic.
>
> Ah yes, I've been around, and yet
> Of all the udders I have met,
> And all that I have seen and felt and tasted,
> Compared to those I saw the day
> I crashed that brassiere display
> Suggests my life has been completely wasted.

For these were busts that stood supreme,
The titulary creme de creme;
They filled me with tit anic tit illations;
I snort and prance, my reason rants,
My morals rip, I rend my pants
Just thinking of those lactic decorations.

For papillary pulchritude
Imbues in me a wanton mood,
My system seethes with fierce, salacious surges;
When I recall those gorgeous gals
And their delightful bosom pals
My spirit howls with indecorous urges.

And through my old rheumatic frame
Primeval passions flash and flame;
Those domes divine are driving me demented,
And if but one in dishabille
I saw them I would die I feel,
But I would perish happy and contented.

9
Not Always Cheap But Usually Nasty . . .

D. H. Lawrence, despite the eroticism of his writing, was something of a prude and frequently intolerant of authors whose ideas did not conform with his own. He even suggested that it was not hard to censor pornography because it was so easily recognisable 'by the insult it offers, invariably, to sex, and to the human spirit'. Ah well, I suppose he's entitled to his opinion.

What is acceptable and what distasteful is something individuals must, as I suggested earlier, decide for themselves. But it isn't simply a question of putting books into categories and dismissing one lot as 'porn', because labels are invariably far too sweeping to encompass everything that fits the definition in theory. At the 'top end' of the market (ie farthest away from the gutter) one might come across the work of talented authors writing to order, usually for money – such as Anaïs Nin (*see* Chapter 7) – or written by them for 'private' consumption. The French poet Paul Verlaine (1844–96) wrote at least three such volumes, described by him as 'sous le manteau' for the enjoyment of his friends. The most apt description of Verlaine's poetry, particularly his earlier work, is *beautiful*; inspiring enough to have fired the imagination of a composer like Debussy, who set to music his *Fêtes galantes*. It is difficult to reconcile anything from the pen of Verlaine with pornography, yet can the deliberate *intent* to excite or stimulate be overlooked just because the writing is of a high standard?

To help you reach your own conclusions, I have included extracts that throw light on the author's intent, style and other points of significance – as well as provide sheer entertainment. Although most of the books discussed in *this* chapter are interesting because of the impression they made in their time on society and the trends they illustrate, few of them have any literary merit. Consequently, I have used fewer extracts; in any case, a large proportion of such pornography is pretty much of a muchness.

The nineteenth century produced an abundance of publications offering sex in all its forms, some of the 'home-grown' variety, others translations of foreign works including classics of sex education such as the *Kama Sutra* from India and *The Perfumed Garden* from Persia.

Fiction was divided between 'conventional' sex and what has been referred to as the 'British' vice – flagellation. (It is not blindly patriotic, I think, to defend the reputations of our ancestors, since there has always been a tendency to attribute 'weaknesses' or 'unmentionables' to foreigners; French leave and French letters, for example, are identified in France as *English* leave and letters.) There is no doubt that flagellation was popular in nineteenth-century England. In the 1860s and 1870s there was a surfeit of books on the fun times to be had with cane or whip, books like *The Merry Order of St Bridget: Personal Recollections of the Use of the Rod* and *The Romance of Chastisement: or Revelations of the School and Bedroom. By an Expert* (!). Even *The Romance of Lust* (1876), which is an everyday story of a young English lad, Charles, had its statutory ration of flagellation, although for most of the time Charles is enjoying less perverted pastimes such as seducing his sisters, making love to an aunt and being sodomised by his uncle.

Since the English, at a time when they could justifiably be called 'imperialists', regarded themselves as a cut above the rest, a popular theme dealt with English girls being 'ravished' by foreigners, particularly the ethnic groups associated with virility. The book that set the trend was *The Lustful Turk* (1828). The solemnity of the full title is amusing:

The Lustful Turk

Part the first. A History Founded on Facts, Containing An interesting Narrative of the cruel fate of the two Young English Ladies, named **Sylvia Carey**, and **Emily Barlow**. Fully explaining How Emily Barlow, and her servant, Eliza Gibbs, on their passage to India, were taken prisoners by an Algerine Pirate, and made a present of to the Dey of Algiers; who, on the very night of their arrival debauched Emily. – Containing also, every particular of the artful plans laid by the Dey, to get possession of the person of **Sylvia Carey** – how he effected his purpose – with the particulars of her becoming a victim to his libidinous desires. Which Recital is also interspersed with the Histories of several other Ladies confined in the Dey's Harem. One of which gives an account of the horrid practices then carrying on in several French and Italian Convents by a society of Monks, established at Algiers, under pretence of redeeming Christian slaves; but who, in reality, carried on an infamous traffic in Young Girls. – Also an account of the sufferings of **Eliza Gibbs**, from the flogging propensities of the Bey of Tunis. With many other curious circumstances, until the reduction of Algiers by Lord Exmouth; by which means these particulars became known. – The whole complied from the Original Letters, by permission of one of the sufferers. Embellished with beautiful engravings. Published in Two Parts. By **An Arcadian**, A 8 [*sic*] The Law Directs; And to be had of all the principal Booksellers in town or country. Price £2.2s. 1828.

In keeping with the best traditions of pornography, the sweet young virgins, once deflowered or 'cruelly ravished', fall passionately in love with their masters who are, of course, highly skilled in the arts of love-making.

> Never, oh never shall I forget the delicious transports that followed the stiff insertion; and then, ah me!, by what thrilling degrees did he, by his luxurious movements, fiery kisses, and strange touches of his hand to the most crimson parts of my body, reduce me to a voluptuous state of insensibility. I blush to say so powerfully did his ravishing instrument stir up nature within me, that by mere instinct I returned him kiss for kiss, responsively meeting his fierce thrusts, until the fury of the pleasure and the ravishment became so overpowering that, unable longer to support the excitement I so luxuriously felt, I fainted in his arms with pleasure.

The 'mix' appealed to readers too and within a year, a second edition was priced at four guineas, a lot of money at that time. The imagery is undoubtedly erotic in places and the writing of an acceptable standard, yet totally predictable. If one defines pornography as the deliberate attempt to arouse before all else, then there can be no doubt this is pornography.

One of the many titles 'inspired' by *The Lustful Turk* was *A Night in a Moorish Harem*, published in Paris in the late 1890s, allegedly by one Lord George Herbert, at the tender age of twenty-three captain of one of His Majesty's ships in the Mediterranean. Although the theme was different (there were no dastardly foreigners ravishing English virgins), the major attraction was again the 'mystery' of the East, although the *action* could have happened anywhere in the world. George swims ashore from his ship, which is anchored off Morocco, and is lured into a harem where he is welcomed with open legs by nine of the beautiful residents. In addition to being good at their work, the lovely ladies are also born story-tellers and fascinate him with their tales of lesbianism and other bits of gossip from the humdrum routine of a harem. Lord George, in common with all heroes of pornography, has the durability of a piston engine, while the ladies are uniformly passionate and responsive to our super-lover.

The most famous pornographic book of the Victorian period was the anonymous autobiography (giving the author the benefit of the doubt that the book is not, in fact, part fiction) *My Secret Life* (1888) in eleven volumes. A handful of rather naïve Bookfinders' clients have at different times asked me to unearth the original set, but since only six copies are supposed to have been run off, the odds are somewhat long! Many edited versions have appeared, and since the repetition even in these is tedious in the extreme, one would find the book almost impossible to read in its original form. The best study of the book, merited only in the context of a sociological history of nineteenth-century England, is contained in *The Other Victorians* by Steven Marcus. Professor Marcus does his job well, but I was surprised when in a footnote he reprimands Gershon Legman, one of the world's foremost authorities on erotica, for his essay on the subject, complaining that he had obviously not read more than three or four volumes! Even the most dedicated member of the dirty-raincoat brigade would surely give up after four.

My Secret Life is an account of the exhausting sexual exploits of the author, 'Walter', a Victorian gentleman whose life seems to have revolved around sex. We are given no clue to 'Walter's' personality and interests beyond his obsession. This could be because of a desire to preserve his anonymity, although it was more likely to have been to avoid wasting space on irrelevancies when he could be cramming every page with as much bizarre sex as possible. No one has ever been able to identify the author, although Legman in *The Horn Book* makes an educated guess at the collector Henry Spencer Ashbee who, under the pseudonym Pisanus Fraxi, compiled the *Index Librorum Prohiborum*, the first bibliography of pornography in English. (In 1879 he added *Centuria Librorum Absconditorum* and six years later *Catena Librorum Tacendorum*.)

Read in isolation, some of the sequences can be erotic, but when one experience follows another without relief over 5,000 pages (the author estimates that he had intercourse with 1,200 women!) the incidents become kaleidoscoped and lose the power to arouse. There are no pretensions to eloquent writing, and his limited vocabulary contributes towards an early sense of *déja vu*. However, one of the author's saving graces is his apparent honesty. One has the impression that some of the incidents reported probably did happen in that way, without the post-coital editing that might have happened with most other diarists. He describes people as they probably were, in an original style, warts and all – like the following account of his relationship with a couple of prostitutes:

> She [Sophy] was exquisitely made, had the loveliest breasts, and from the nape of her neck to the sole of her feet was as white as snow. Her features were good, her eyes blue, and yet she looked like a fool, and when she laughed was like an idiot. Her laugh was a vulgar, idiotic, coarse, offensive chuckle; she opened her mouth quite wide (it was large with splendid teeth), and she rolled her head from side to side. . . .
>
> Of all the women I ever had, none had so soft, so voluptuous a cunt. . . . Sophy shivered, quivered, but not noisily, and heaved gently; her cunt went clip, clip, suck, suck, in a wonderful way towards her crisis, and then with a gentle heave of her belly and arse, she seemed as if she wished to get my whole body up her, and with an 'Ahaa-my dear man-aha, aha,' she subsided. . . . She liked me and used to patter out in her ugly, hoarse, coarse, vulgar voice, bawdy words, and coarse but loving expressions. Nelly, watching us, used then to say, 'Sophy–what are you at?' but it did not stop her. Never have I had more completely voluptuous fucking as far as mere cunt was concerned, but that was all; I was sick of the sight of her directly our bodies unjoined.
>
> I saw both girls daily for nearly a fortnight, and Sophy had my

seminal libations more frequently than Nelly—but I could not talk to her; her language was indescribably common and coarse, and whether eating, drinking, speaking, washing or even pissing, her vulgarity and idiocy were intolerable. She was a magnificent bit of fucking flesh but nothing more. . . .

At the time that *My Secret Life* was being prepared for publication, a talented young Irish journalist was gaining the experience of 'life' that would one day produce the twentieth-century 'sequel', his own autobiography *My Life and Loves.* The young man was Frank Harris (1856–1931), who had gone to the United States when he was fifteen and 'graduated' the hard way, through a variety of jobs from bootblack to lawyer, in the best American tradition. Coming to England, he entered journalism for which he had a natural aptitude, subsequently becoming editor of *The Fortnightly Review*, *The Saturday Review* and *Vanity Fair*. In between he was editor of the London *Evening News* at the age of twenty-seven, at a period when circulation related directly to the dynamism of the editor – and the paper's readership soared under Harris's mantle. As a biographer his studies included books on Shakespeare, Shaw and Wilde.

Opinions about *My Life and Loves* are divided between those who dismiss the books (the first published in Germany in 1922, and subsequent volumes in France until 1927) as pornography, and those who regard them as the work of a courageously outspoken writer of integrity. It must be said that the respected Doctors Eberhart and Phyllis Kronhausen in *Pornography and the Law* defend Harris, suggesting that had he written the autobiography in post-Kinseyan America, he might have had a better chance of being understood and appreciated. My own feeling is that the book can be judged only on an understanding of the author's intention, and that is something we shall never know for certain.

Harris, the connoisseur of sex, is as explicit as his Victorian counterpart 'Walter', but there the comparison ends. Having expressed the view that the earlier work had some value as a social history, I feel that Harris falls between two stools. I suspect that, at a time when his career was on the slide and he needed money, Harris set out to write what his business experience told him was a highly marketable piece of erotica. His 'secret' on the *Evening News* forty years before had been to sell blood, thunder and sex – a formula other newspaper tycoons have since copied – and when he started on his memoirs, that was probably at the forefront of his mind.

If that was so, the plan misfired, because the only people who made any money from the first volume were the pirate publishers who cashed in on the fuss that greeted its publication. The reaction of his contemporaries was uniformly critical, and I don't think this can be blamed entirely on the moral climate of the 1920s. One of the very few who remained loyal to some extent was George Bernard Shaw, although Mrs Shaw is reported to have burned their copy. A pity because without the heavy lacing of sex, the *Life* makes interesting reading.

Perhaps I'm being unfair to Harris, but if he was consciously turning out pornography in the guise of biography, the subterfuge would not have been unprecedented. Publishers have frequently tried to cloud the issue by professing some altruistic motive. In the *Memoirs of Dolly Morton*, the publisher Charles Carrington raised his eyes to Heaven, and protested that he was offering the world an account of a 'woman's part in the struggle to free the slaves' in America. That it was written by his friend George Grassal (under the pseudonym Hughes Rebell), a known enthusiast for flagellation, that most of the book is concerned with whipping and that the title-page indicates it was published in Philadelphia for the Society of Bibliophiles when it was really produced in Paris (in 1904), are all conveniently forgotten. Dolly, the heroine, is, of course, witness to the regular beating of women slaves, is whipped herself and is generally involved in a variety of sexual activities. Later, as a 'madame', she helps to organise, as well as participate in, some very naughty goings-on. Yet part of the publisher's blurb reads:

Publisher's Notice
Concerning
Foreign Pirates, Private Books,
and
Negro Emancipation

The pages of 'Dolly Morton' are not meant for the eyes of 'babes and sucklings' – its tropical descriptions would scorch their weakling sight and unsettle their wavering soul. These private memoirs elucidate certain curious vagaries of the ever-changing human mind which are good to be known, though only by scholars and accredited bibliophiles, who will be careful to place the precious volume on the top shelves of their locked book-case.

A book of this kind can only escape the charge of immorality when kept out of the reach of the multitude by the prohibitiveness of its price and the limited number of the edition. Upon the seared senses of the man of the world or the trained mind of the thinker, it can have no pernicious effect. But if addressed *virginibus puerisque* and peddled from house to house, it becomes a weapon of the deadliest kind.

The chemist is allowed to dispense poisons under certain conditions; the lawyer, judge, and doctor, to enquire into matters wisely hid from the common ken, and such a work as 'The Memoirs of Dolly Morton' falls, we opine, under the same rules and restrictions.

These are some of the reasons why we decided to issue this fascinating production – a human document in the truest sense.

There are also other reasons of nearly equal importance, but, which concern more particularly the subscribers to this work.

It may not be generally known that shortly after Sir Richard F. Burton brought out 'The Thousand Nights and a Night', a conspiracy was entered into by certain foreign individuals to reprint his work and issue it on the Continent at a lower price, to the great detriment of course, of Burton's original edition. The book had not been copyrighted in England. Hence the danger.

The rumour of the little 'game' *en train de cuire* came to the translator's ears, and steps were at once taken legally to protect his literary property.

This trick of reprinting privately-issued and uncopyrighted books is often resorted to by unscrupulous dealers in obscenity. Honourable gentlemen of this 'kidney' in Brussels and Amsterdam reprinted the 'Ananga Ranga', 'Kama Sutra', and other books of the Cosmopolis Society directed by Burton and Arbuthnot; and the reprinting goes on, in a similar way, on the clandestine presses of London and Paris.

A work like the present for instance, issued to subscribers at a high price and in a limited number, would, if it were not legally registered, be immediately seized upon by the 'filth vendors', struck off by thousands on common paper and offered at half or quarter the price of the original, with no other object than to turn over money by pandering to the erotic tastes of libertines and debauched men.

> Thus a work, issued as a literary curiosity, and because possessing a certain pathological meaning to students, is used as an instrument of shameful gain and degradation, with the result that the bibliophile and subscriber (living at a distance and unsuspecting the fraud), imagines on seeing the advertisement of the bastard reprint that he has been overcharged by his own bookseller. Of course, the reprint more often than not bristles with textual errors from the fact that the literary pirate is absolutely ignorant of the English language, and would never dream of going to the expense of employing a competent proofreader. In fact, in many cases, only half the original text is given – while the full title is preserved – in order further to cut down the expenses of the ignoble and dishonest reproduction.

If the reader has any doubts at this stage, he is satisfied by chapter sub-headings such as this:

> A Rabelaisian banquet of nude damsels. —A shocking orgie. —Ten naked waitresses and their bashfulness. —Hot viands and bottom-spanking escapades. —Original racing in the corridors, and the inevitable sequel.

Dolly may have been phoney, but one of the most prolific of the genuine American authors of the second half of the nineteenth century was George Thompson, as the following title page indicates:

> *The Delights of Love*
> or, The Lady Libertine. Being the Adventures of an Amorous Widow.
>
> By GEORGE THOMPSON ('Greenhorn'), author of *The Bridal Chamber*, *Venus in Boston*, *The Gay Deceiver*, *Jack Harold*, and one hundred other popular tales. J. H. FARRELL, 15 Ann Street, New York.

Thompson's stories are concerned solely with sex, and he wastes few words on background, atmosphere, characterisation and even plot. Yet few are truly pornographic by today's standards. Worse, most of them have the sickly saccharine flavour of the following extract. Handsome hero and beautiful heroine have been admiring a painting of Venus and Adonis. They are overwhelmed:

> The eyes of both Julia and Eugene now simultaneously turned

upon this exciting gem of art, and, like electricity, there passed from one to the other a bursting declaration of their mutual wishes.

'Be my Adonis!' murmured the lady libertine, as she pantingly sank into the arms of the eager youth, who whispered, as he pressed her yielding form to his wildly throbbing heart —

'I am yours, my Venus!'. . .

It is a great pity, we know, and the reader may blame us for it; but we are here reluctantly compelled to drop the curtain.

One entire hour was passed by the lovers in the enjoyment of such ecstatic blisses as the divine passion of *Love* can alone afford, when it has thrown off all artificial trammels, and suffers *Nature* to reign supreme. . . .

Thompson did not usually apologise to his readers by 'dropping the curtain', but no matter how torried the love scene or orgy, he could be relied upon to remain uniformly coy. In *Fanny Greeley, or, Confessions of a Free-love Sister Written by Herself*, his heroine is beautiful (naturally) an orphan (of course) and rich (she has to be). On leaving school and with nowhere to go, Fanny throws herself upon one Diamond Dunstable, a lecturer with whom she has fallen in love. Dunstable may sound like an idiot, but he's no fool:

As he spoke, he proceeded with no unpractised hand to unfasten the various hooks and eyes, and buttons, ribbons, and lacings with which dressmakers are wont to incase us. When at length, passive and palpitating beneath his soft, caressing hands, I found myself with only one garment, which far from clinging round my shoulders fell from them and revealed my arms and bust, I, to hide my blushes and myself from his kindling glance, could but throw myself into his arms and clinging close to his breast hide my face in his bosom.

He pressed me to him, he disengaged my feet from the fallen garments which embarrassed them, and laying me by his side he slowly passed his hand up and down the spine, over my bosom, and down my arms, till my whole frame thrilled beneath his touch, and I could not tell whether it was pain or pleasure that I felt.

His eyes were immovably fixed on mine and mine were fascinated by their glance. I had no power to move, a dreamy, intoxicated feeling came over me; my breath came quick and panting through my parted lips: I was as though in a trance–dead I seemed to the outward world–I had no thought of the past, of the future; indeed no distinct speculation of the present, yet I was in a state of the most unspeakable, most ecstatic enjoyment.

Perfectly passive and unresisting thus magnetized, was I when my lover wheeling me on the sofa to the bed gently laid me on it, and satisfied by the holy rites of love the passions he had excited to the highest pitch.

Another prolific writer on this side of the Atlantic was Edward Sellon, a former Indian Army officer, who never seemed to settle down and who befriended the publishers of pornography for whom he wrote with such success. In terms of 'staying power' his most popular book was *The New Ladies' Tickler, or The Adventures of Lady Lovesport and the Audacious Harry* (1866), which, C. M. Bowra in *Memories 1898–1939* recalls, was read in the trenches of the Western Front by British soldiers fifty years later.

Sellon was a restless man and eventually shot himself in a London hotel. In his remarkable bibliography of pornography, Ashbee (Pisanus Fraxi) paid tribute to him: 'Here then is the melancholy career, terminating in suicide at the early age of 48 years, of a man by no means devoid of talent, and undoubtedly capable of better things.' It is generally considered that Sellon's best work was *The Ups and Downs of Life* (1867, the manuscript was completed shortly before his death), which is said to be autobiographical and makes interesting reading for that reason alone. Sellon deals with his ten years of army service in India and with his sexual relations with Indian women, whom he much preferred to European women, with whom he was also widely experienced. Back in England he gets married and resigns his commission, which may well have been the root of his problem, but the marriage is strained and he is discovered in an affair with a pretty parlourmaid. The following scene sums up the constant tension in his life, even though the violence has sexual undertones, and Sellon is soon making love to an ardent mistress and now acquiescent wife. His wife has discovered the affair; she attacks him physically, biting, scratching and kicking, and he asks if she had ever seen Shakespeare's *The Taming of the Shrew*:

No answer.

'Well, my angel, I'm going to tame you.' She renewed her bites and kicks, and called me all the miscreants and vile scoundrels under the sun. I continued to hold her in a vice of iron. Thus we continued till six o'clock.

'If it is your will and pleasure to expose yourself to the servants,' said I, 'pray do, I have no objection but I will just observe that John will come in presently to clear away the luncheon and lay the cloth for dinner.' A torrent of abuse was the only answer.

'You brute,' she said, 'you have bruised my wrists black and blue.'

'Look at my hands, my precious angel, and my shins are in still worse condition.'

By and by there was a rap at the door, 'Come in,' said I. John appeared— 'Take no notice of us, John, but attend to your business.'

John cleared away the luncheon and laid the cloth for dinner. Exit John.

'Oh, Edward, you do hurt my wrists so.'

'My ear and face are still burning with the blow you gave me, my hands are torn to pieces with your tiger teeth, and will not be fit to be seen for a month, and as to my shins, my drawers are saturated with blood,' said I.

'Let me go! let me go directly, wretch!' and again she bit, kicked and struggled.

'Listen to me,' said I, 'there are 365 days in the year, but by God! if there were 3,605, I hold you till you apologize in the manner and way I told you, and even then, I shall punish you likewise for the infamous way you have behaved.' She sulked for another half hour, but did not bite or kick any more. I never relaxed my grasp, or the sternness of my countenance. My hands were streaming with blood, some of the veins were opened, her lap was full of blood, it was a frightful scene.

At length she said, 'Edward, I humbly ask your pardon for the shameful way I have treated you, I apologize for the blow I gave you, I forgive you for any injury you have done me, I promise to be docile and humble in future, and I beg—I beg,' she sobbed, 'your forgiveness.'

I released her hands, pulled the bell violently, told John to run immediately for Dr Monson, (the family physician,) and fell fainting on the floor. I had lost nearly a pint of blood from the wounds inflicted by the panther. When I recovered my senses, I was lying on the sofa, my hands enveloped in strapping plaster and bandages, as were also my shins. Ellen [*sic*] and my wife knelt at my feet crying, while Monson kept pouring port wine down my throat. 'Could you eat a little,' said he kindly.

'Gad, yes,' said I, 'I'm awfully hungry, bring dinner, John.'

Later:

I had one of my bandaged hands up Emma's clothes while he was saying this, and was feeling her lovely young cunny. It was nuts to crack for me. Dr Monson gone, I rang the bell, 'John, you and the servants can go to bed,' said I. John cast an enquiring glance at Madam and Emma, bowed and retired.

I asked Emma for my cigar-case, as for Augusta, I did not notice her. I lit a cigar, and drawing Emma on my knee, sat before the fire and smoked. 'You can go to bed, Augusta,' said I, as if she was the servant and Emma the wife, 'I shall not want you any more.' The humbled woman took her candle, and wishing us both good night, went to bed.

'Oh, Edward,' said poor little Emma, 'what a dreadful woman she is, she nearly killed you, you nearly bled to death! Dr Monson said two of the great veins at the back of each hand had been opened by her teeth, and that if she had not given in when she did, you would have bled to death.'

'But here I am all alive, my sweet.'

'But you won't have me to-night, mind.'

'Won't I though!'

'Now, Edward! pray don't, you are too weak!'

'Then this will give me strength,' said I, and I drank at a draught a tumbler of Carbonell's old Port. I made her drink another glass, and then we lay down on the couch together. I fucked her twice, and then in each other's arms we fell asleep.

During World War II, a number of publishers in the United Kingdom, trying to cater for what they thought was a demand for tough American-style thrillers, evolved a new genre devoted almost entirely to sadism and violence. Two of the forerunners were *Lady Don't Turn Over* by Darcy Glinto and *Miss Callaghan Comes to Grief* by James Hadley Chase, whose genuine talent was eventually recognised in more respectable circles. In 1942, both books (among others) were prosecuted and, following a trial at the Old Bailey, publishers and authors were fined.

Nothing in either story is allowed to interrupt the constant flow of torture, rape and the most extreme violence. One of the other common features of the plots is the white-slave traffic, and incredibly the defence for *Miss Callaghan* had the temerity to suggest that the book was an exposé of the evils of white slavery in the same way that *Uncle Tom's Cabin* had opened people's eyes to black slavery! Shades of *Dolly Morton*! But if these books were considered beyond the pale, there were countless imitations treading perilously close to the borderline, not far removed from the slime of horror comics.

Within a few years the style seemed relatively tame and the scene was set for the introduction of an even viler pornography, lurid paperbacks sold in the United States under the series title *Nights of Horror*. In 1955, four Brooklyn teenagers were horribly tortured before being drowned by a gang whose eighteen-year-old leader was obviously 'inspired' by the paperbacks he read from cover to cover. A year later the books were banned, after a New York judge related the de Sade type horrors featured in the series.

The author of *Seduction of the Innocents*, Dr Frank Wertham, had already drawn attention to the explosion of horror comics after World War II, pointing out that in 1937 in the United States there were only eighteen crime comic titles, but less than twenty years later they dominated the vast, multi-million dollar comic market. Luckily, in the United Kingdom youngsters were not exposed to such a wide variety of magazines, although what there was was bad enough. Apart from a surfeit of sex and violence of the most extreme sort, the common feature of these comics was the development of neo-fascist philosophies expounded by pre-war English writers, such as Dornford Yates and Sapper (C. H. McNeile), featuring the superiority of the WASP over all others and the justification of brutality in the war against 'inferior races'.

10
Artists, Publishers and Collectors

Illustrations can serve more than one purpose; they may complement the printed word, or they may completely overshadow the author's work, which is why some antiquarian books are collected solely for their illustrations. Or they can be used merely to assist readers who have difficulty with words! Standards, therefore as well as styles vary as much as in writing itself. Books may include works of art right down to lavatory-wall graffiti.

I've discussed the relationship between erotica and pornography at length, and to be consistent one has to apply the same criteria to art. One must at least start by relating illustrations and sculpture to the age for which they were created. Some pre-Christian religions, for example, worshipped the sex organs as the source of creation, so that a visual tribute to the phallus or the breasts was no more offensive than any symbol of a 'modern' deity, whether it be a cross or a clenched fist.

Admittedly, few of the artists who gained a reputation for erotica had aesthetic tributes in mind when they painted the pictures for which they are now celebrated. Yet for all their sensuality, few would deny that some of the work of, for example, Gulio Romano (1497–1546) – whose drawings for Pietro Aretino's *Sonetti Lussuriosi* got him into hot water – is beautiful as well as erotic. Early in his career Romano was chief assistant to Raphael, working on frescos in the Vatican, and his more conventional work can be seen and appreciated today at some of the world's major galleries, but many of these paintings have hedonistic qualities that hint strongly at the artist's talent for erotica.

In 1589, the Carracci family, also associated with Aretino's sonnets, fostered the trend towards total frankness when they established an academy of art, *Academia degli incamminati*, intended to counteract the 'artificiality' of Michelangelo.

Two Carracci brothers, Agostino (1557–1602) and Annibale (1560–1609), are particularly identified with erotica – the former, principally an engraver, being even more explicit than Romano; Annibale, the greatest of a very talented family, is known particularly for his uninhibited decoration of the ceiling and enormous gallery of the Cardinal Farnese palace in Rome. Had they been reproduced in book form, the scenes of Roman gods at play in what might be termed 'naked abandon' would probably have invoked storms of protest at different periods.

Styles tell us as much about artists as they do about writers. William Hogarth (1697–1764) turned his back on romanticism when he chose to deal with moral issues of the day, declaring that he treated his subjects as a dramatic writer: 'My picture is my stage, and men and women players.' He established himself as England's most popular artist with the publication of six etchings entitled 'The Harlot's Progress'. Coarse, but frighceningly realistic, the pictures told the story of London's evil influence on a young country girl, Mary, forcing her into prostitution, prison, eventual ruin (which is what made the subject acceptable) and finally death through syphilis. The brothel scene, especially, leaves little to the imagination. Twelve thousand sets were sold, but the success of pirate publishers induced Hogarth to fight for copyright protection, and through his efforts an Act was passed in 1735. Hogarth followed his success with other studies of licentiousness, notably 'The Rake's Progress' and 'Marriage à la Mode'.

Hogarth inspired another outstanding caricaturist, James Gillray (1757–1815), who also produced a number of book illustrations. Although his subjects were mainly political, a number of drawings depicted people's least agreeable 'personal' habits, and many are more vulgar than erotic. A fair proportion of these satirical works were suppressed because they might cause offence, but the subjects also included flagellation. A former actor, Gillray often displayed a theatrical flamboyance in his work, and one picture featured the Empress Josephine and Madame Talian dancing in the nude in front of Barras. His most erotic work was probably 'The Wedding Night'.

Gillray's most famous contemporary, Thomas Rowlandson (1756–1827), started as a serious painter but got into the habit of spending more than he earned and was obliged to tackle more widely appealing subjects to boost his income. In common with Hogarth and Gillray, he is remembered for capturing the lifestyle of the age in which he lived, but the work of Rowlandson is generally more exuberant and good-humoured. Much of it is openly erotic, and the collection of Henry Spencer Ashbee (Pisanus Fraxi), bequeathed to the British Library, contained over a hundred plates, including those from the posthumous publication *Pretty Little Games for Young Girls and Gentlemen* (1845), with Rowlandson's verse accompanying his illustrations.

The ten plates contained in *Pretty Little Games* were incorporated in book form for the first time by Joseph Camden Hotten in 1872 in an edition limited to a hundred copies and priced at £3 10s. Each was totally explicit but kept from being pornographic by Rowlandson's *joie de vivre*. Hotten attempted to add a note of respectability by including his own very sober artistic appraisal of each study, some even quite critical. The plates, mostly featuring the various sexual positions, are entitled: 'The Willing Fair, or any Way to Please', 'The Country Squire new Mounted', 'The Toss Off', 'Rural Felicity or Love in a Chaise', 'The Sanctified Sinner', 'The Wanton Frolic', 'The Curious Wanton' and 'The Hairy Prospect or the Devil in a Fright'. Another, 'New Feats of Horsemanship', features a huntsman 'riding' a young woman, with both astride his horse. Rowlandson's companying commentary reads:

Well mounted on a mettle steed,
Famed for his strength as well as speed,
Corrinna and her favourite buck
Are pleas'd to have a flying f--k,
While o'er the downs the courser strains,
With fiery eye and loosened reins,
Around his neck her arms she flings,
Behind her buttocks move like springs,
While Jack keeps time to every motion,
And pours in love's delicious potion.

'The Larking Cull' is a bedroom scene, with a young lover standing over his mistress:

While on the bed the nymphs reclined,
Damons resolv'd to please his mind.

His generation tube he shows.
Between her swelling breasts it goes.
His fingers to her touch hole sent,
Alas to give her small content.
A larger thing would give more pleasure,
She always loves to have full measure.
And who for greater joys do hunt
Than rising bubbies and a C--t.

A number of authorities maintain that another even more famous caricaturist, George Cruikshank (1792–1878), a name often linked with Dickens, also tried his hand at erotica – providing the illustrations for an edition of *Fanny Hill* – but extensive enquiries have failed to substantiate that claim. His father, Isaac, is also alleged to have illustrated at least one book of pornography.

To some extent, I suppose, we associate erotic drawings of quality with satirists, because they were expected to shock; yet many famous 'straight' artists have turned their talents in this direction, and perhaps the most surprising, someone especially loved by the English, was J. M. W. Turner (1775–1851). In an unsubstantiated anecdote in Volume II of *My Life and Loves*, Frank Harris retells John Ruskin's account of what happened after he was asked by the National Gallery to sort through Turner's paintings and sketches, which had been bequeathed to the nation. Ruskin confided to Harris that he was so shocked by the contents of one large portfolio that he *burned* what he described as 'scrofulous' work. The subjects of most of this were apparently the external sex organs of women, and it transpired that Turner had spent many weekends at Wapping painting 'sailors' women' (whatever that means!). Since they were destroyed, we shall never know what Ruskin meant by 'scrofulous'; presumably they were not just anatomical studies.

There was an abundance of talent on the continent of Europe, including François Boucher (1703–70), a friend and protégé of Mme de Pompadour, and his pupil, Jean Fragonard (1732–1806), whose reputation for erotica encouraged Madame du Barry to commission a series entitled 'Progress of Love' for her new house. It seems she did not find them acceptable – although whether they were too erotic or insufficiently so is not clear – and they are now preserved for posterity in a New York museum. An outstanding talent in this sphere was the Belgian-born Parisian Felicien Rops (1833–98), a friend of Baudelaire, with whose work he has much in common. They shared a remarkable and original talent for portraying life (especially debauchery) with rich imagery and a cynicism that contrasted sharply with their more romantic moods. Rops had a surrealist style long before surrealism was 'discovered'. His paintings and illustrations for books – title-pages were one of his specialities – were highly original, sometimes pornographic, but always exciting. A more familiar name is Toulouse-Lautrec (1864–1901), whose fascinating life and stunted growth merited the attention of Hollywood some years ago. Known for his habit of taking his easel to the subject, rather than restricting himself to a studio, Toulouse-Lautrec relied heavily on actresses and prostitutes for his models. Many well-known paintings feature nude studies, but he also painted subjects rather less acceptable in most societies.

In the Far East too, erotic literature had plenty of illustrators. Regarded today as one of the greatest masters of the art was the Japanese artist Utamaro (1753–1806), whose *The Twelve Hours of the Green Houses* follows a day in the life of a grand courtesan of the day. Japanese art is, however, rather more subtle than western, and his work, while interesting and quite charming, is not as sexually stimulating as that of many European artists.

One of the names most eagerly sought by collectors of antiquarian books today is that of Aubrey Vincent Beardsley, who had produced over five hundred remarkable black-and-white drawings before his death from tuberculosis at the age of twenty-six in 1898. His best-known works include the illustrated edition of Oscar Wilde's *Salome*. Anticipating the film-makers of the twentieth century, Beardsley invariably produced two versions of the erotica he tackled, and 'The Toilet of Salome', for example, showed the lady and her attendant undressed in the original tableau, yet dressed in the published version. Naturally, the undressed version became the one in demand.

In 1896 Beardsley provided the drawings for a privately printed edition of Aristophanes' *Lysistrata* and when he was dying two years later he wrote to the publisher asking for all copies to be destroyed; but like Rochester 200 years before, he was asking the impossible. Another of his masterpieces, one for which he also provided the text, was *The Story of Venus and Tannhauser*, published in expurgated form in the magazine *The Savoy*, but in the original form after his death in a specially produced book, limited to 250 copies (1907).

Without the specialist publisher and collector, there would be no author or illustrator, so let's pause to reflect on the type of man who fits this category. I've already mentioned Edmund Curll, but in the nineteenth century – in parallel with the wave of prudery – there was an enormous demand for erotica and pornography. Double standards were now not only acceptable but usually the rule, and several men specialised quite openly – with mixed fortunes.

The most defiantly professional of them all was William Dugdale, who came to London from Lancashire as a young man and ran up what must be a record total of a dozen prison sentences in the cause of pornography. Dugdale, a refreshingly honest scoundrel, gambled for high stakes. Among the dozens of successful titles he published were *The Romance of Chastisement, or The Revelations of Miss Darcy* (1866), with eight coloured lithographs, which should not be confused with *The Romance of Chastisement, or Revelations of the School and Bedroom, by an Expert* (1870, published by John Camden Hotten), and *Don Leon*, purported to have been written by Byron. But Dugdale produced in volume, necessary to offset the large losses sustained when the police regularly raided his premises as part of a running battle and confiscated most of what they could find. The conclusion must be that he was quite successful, but the 'rewards' for his headstrong behaviour had to be offset by his long spells in prison, where he finally died in 1868.

Charles Carrington (real name Paul Ferdinando) came to an even more unpleasant end, dying in a lunatic asylum in 1922, blind and ravaged by syphilis. Carrington was rather more underhand than Dugdale, choosing to operate from the relative safety of Paris, although even there he quickly became regarded as an undesirable alien. Nevertheless he was devious enough to wriggle free of two attempts to deport him.

From humble beginnings, Carrington 'graduated' when he was sixteen years old to selling books in London's Farringdon market – only a stone's throw from what became a mecca for bibliophiles, the bookstalls in Farringdon Road. Having developed an interest in books and extended his knowledge, he started to publish 'good' (that is, expensive) erotica, which gradually became more and more pornographic, so that HM Customs, watching for prohibited goods coming from the Continent, classified undesirable material as '*any* books published by Carrington'.

A great rival of Carrington was Leonard Smithers, a Sheffield solicitor who moved to London to find the action and became a bookseller! Having become friendly with a number of writers, he moved into publishing, courageously operating from London in the 1890s. His list of quality erotica included the works of Oscar Wilde and Aubrey Beardsley. Smithers was a strange man, ostensibly a rough diamond, yet capable of translating from Latin and Greek, and wily enough to escape prosecution through devious tactics, usually copied by his contemporaries.

John Camden Hotten (1832–73) was one publisher who managed to protect his reputation, and that nineteenth-century authority on pornography, Henry Spencer Ashbee, described him as 'almost the only respectable English publisher of tabooed literature'. This was largely because Hotten had gained in stature by bringing out Swinburne's *Poems & Ballads* (1866), after the poet's usual publisher, Edward Moxon, had cold feet over a possible prosecution. A talented man (confident enough to provide the commentary mentioned earlier for Rowlandson's erotic prints), he wrote *A History of Signboards*, which is still in demand today. He must also be given credit for introducing the works of such American writers as Mark Twain and Edgar Allan Poe. But for all his apparent respectability, Hotten did not hesitate to publish questionable material such as *The Merry Muses* (the 'Burns' collection), and *The Merry Order of St Bridget; Personal Recollections of the Use of the Rod* (1857) by Margaret Anson (in fact, a man!). Incidentally, it was Hotten's publishing business that (after his death) provided the foundations for the present-day publishers Chatto & Windus.

In our own century, the outstanding publisher of erotica and pornography has been Maurice Girodias, a very different character from his nineteenth-century counterparts. Girodias, son of an English publisher who had also tried to buck the system, has always been at the forefront of the fight against censorship, believing that without censorship there would be no pornography to speak of. He is best known for founding and editing the short-lived Paris-based, English-language Olympia Press, which brought new dimensions not only to erotica but to modern literature in general. Writing in a preface to *The Best of Olympia* (1966), Mr Girodias gives us an inkling of his personality and his philosophy. Don't be put off by what appears to be a hard-luck story – what he later in the piece dismisses as 'whining' – because here we have space for only a short extract which hardly does him justice:

> When I began publishing 'Olympia' in 1961 my idea was to create a house organ of a kind, and its function was mainly to attract and help in the discovery of new talent. But I was working against insuperable odds, and each issue of 'Olympia' marked an important date in my struggle against fate. In fact only four issues of that so-called monthly were printed between 1961 and 1963, and each one was at the cost of Herculean efforts. . . .
>
> When I decided to publish that magazine I had already been the pet victim of the French censors for five or six years – although I was only publishing books in English, which they could not read. Years earlier my original edition of *Lolita*, of *The Ginger Man*, of *The Story of O*, *Fanny Hill*, of *Our Lady of the Flowers* and of *Candy* had been banned among dozens of other books of varying importance. I had bravely counter-attacked my censors in the Paris courts, and I had even won encouraging victories in the early stages; but after 1958 no hope was left to justify my resistance. The last judgements issued by the highest court in France, the Conseil d'Etat, made it quite clear: I was a bum, I had no business making things difficult for the French police who were only doing their duty; and people like me were a disgrace, in any case, and I was giving a bad name to France, to *le rayonnement de la culture française à l'étranger*, and all that.
>
> Naturally I wrote to the Minister of the Interior, Monsieur Frey, to protest against what seemed to be an error. No answer. Then I went to see an official of that ministry, who acts as adviser in matters involving the Press and publishers. He listened to me with an expression of complacent boredom, and when I asked him whether he thought le Ministre would perchance suppress the ban, he simply answered that he did not think he would. I was beginning to lose patience, and I asked if he personally thought that such a ban was fair and whether it was not a rather unseemly restriction against freedom of the Press. He merely smiled, absently, as if he was thinking of something else of more

substantial importance, such as the menu of his last meal. I got quite angry and asked with a shaking voice if the magazine had not been banned simply because I was its publisher. And at last I got his attention: 'But of course, cher Monsieur,' he exclaimed with unfeigned joviality, 'c'est evident! You know very well that you are not well noted by this administration, so you should not be surprised if your magazine has been suppressed as a matter of routine. And now if you will allow me . . . ' he concluded, half getting-up and showing me the door with a perfunctory flourish.

Girodias merits a place in the history of literature because of the opportunities he gave to emerging writers. He acted not only as literary editor, but as advisor and promoter too, being usually obliged to give his writers pseudonyms. These *he* insisted on choosing for fear of being landed with a libel suit from the indignant owner of a household name.

The third corner of the triangle is of course the collector, primarily the people who were affluent enough to amass libraries of significant size. Henry Spencer Ashbee (1834–1900) was perhaps the outstanding example. I described him earlier as the greatest authority on the subject; his interest in erotica and pornography was almost obsessional. Yet Ashbee was not the sort of man one imagines dressed in a shabby raincoat and drooling over his purchases. A fairly typical Victorian businessman and parent, he was utterly clinical in his approach. Because of his success in business he was able to retire early and could afford to buy anything he considered of interest. He travelled extensively for the purpose – as far afield as China, Japan, Africa and the United States, which is impressive by nineteenth-century standards.

When he died, a library of more than 15,000 specialist volumes (many of them extremely rare) was bequeathed to the British Museum which, it has been suggested, was not wildly enthusiastic about accepting them. Fortunately, Ashbee had another very desirable collection – his more public obsession: the illustrated editions of Cervantes' *Don Quixote*. His desire to donate *that* depended on the Museum's accepting the former!

Ashbee's library had been enriched by the collection of a friend, Frederick Hankey, who specialised in books on sadism and actually

EX EROTICIS
J. F. K.

EX·LIBRIS·EROTICIS
K·J·OBRÁTIL

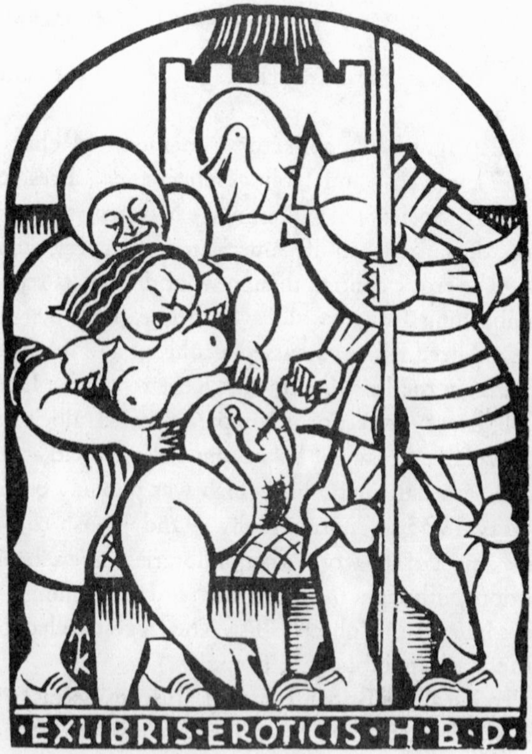

Erotic bookplates offer a challenge to collectors. For obvious reasons they are difficult to find – an added incentive. This sample group represents the designs of Valentin le Campion (France) *left*, Karel Simunek (Czechoslovakia) *below left*, and *above* Max Kislinger (Austria).

chose to live in Paris because of his strange obsession with the life and works of the Marquis de Sade. The son of an English general and cousin to the Governor of the Bank of England, Hankey is described with some revulsion in the de Goncourts' *Journal* in an anecdote recalling how he had shown his collection to one of them. Talking about exotic bindings, he described why he was waiting for a binding to be made from the skin of a young girl and how it would have been prepared. I've been unable to ascertain whether or not he achieved that ambition, but clearly he was a distinctly unappealing individual.

Richard Monckton-Milnes (1809–85), the first Baron Houghton, an MP and editor and biographer of Keats, was a collector on a grand scale who used Hankey to do much of his legwork in Paris; many of the purchases were smuggled into England by various devious means, including the use of Government diplomatic bags.

More distinguished collectors include Michael Sadleir (1888–1957), novelist and bibliographer, and a President of the Bibliographical Society; J. Pierpoint Morgan and Henry E. Huntington, the larger-than-life American millionaires, who were less interested in the erotic content than in what the books represented in terms of publishing antiquity and who bequeathed their libraries to museums. Dr Alfred Kinsey amassed a collection of 15,000 volumes which are now in the Institute for Sex Research at the University of Indiana. The Kinsey collection is comparable with (albeit larger) than the 12,000-volume library of Dr Magnus Hirschfield at the Institut für Sexualwissenschaft in Berlin, which was publicly burned by the Nazis in May 1933 as 'pornography – and Jewish to boot!'

Of course, most of the world's major libraries have a 'behind closed doors' section, although the numbers tend to diminish as books constantly come off the 'obscene' list. The largest collection appears to be in the Vatican Library in Rome.

The collection at the British Library (Museum) seems to have been whittled down dramatically over the years, considering the size of the Ashbee bequest. Called the Arcana collection (from the Latin word for mystery), the books are housed in what is called the Private Case. In similar vein, the Library of Congress in Washington calls its collection Delta, from the Greek symbol for the female sex organ. Typically, the name given by the French to the collection in the Bibliothèque Nationale in Paris is more dramatic – L'Enfer (Hell)!

11
What Turns You On?

If sexuality is associated with the *physical* state, then eroticism, which, like beauty, lies in the eye and mind of the beholder, is principally an aesthetic quality. It is what our *senses* do with the printed word that determines our attitude. I've dealt at length with what might be called 'conventional' erotic books, although I hope in most cases there has been nothing ordinary about the works featured. But there are people who get more sexual stimulation from *un*conventionally erotic books, from Gothic horror stories, for example.

D. H. Lawrence considered *Jane Eyre* pornographic, and I can see what he means. Miss Eyre symbolises to me the hypocrisy inherent in so many of us. Relatively few admit to reading or enjoying erotica or porn, yet a 1979 report by the Library Association, dealing with books stolen or 'lost' from libraries (as high as one per cent of stocks every year), disclosed that the two subjects most in demand were cars, mainly manuals, and sex – again manuals!

This hypocrisy or prudery has always been reflected in a variety of ways. The widely travelled Sir Richard Burton (1821–90) aided by his brilliance as a linguist, became an authority on erotica of the East. One of his outstanding achievements was a scholarly translation of *The Arabian Nights' Entertainment*, yet his translation of the *Kama Sutra*, and the diaries he had kept for twenty-seven years of his fascinating life, were among the literary works burned by his disapproving widow who thought she was protecting his reputation. The novel *The Greek Passion* provides another example of this hypocrisy; Nikos Kazantzakis described in a homosexual context a 'beautiful young Turkish boy'. In Germany, the translation changed the child into a girl – to be on the safe side. A correction was never made.

That may have been an extreme example of playing safe by

anticipating the censor, when he might have remained blissfully ignorant. Throughout the book I've been less than kind to censors, whoever they may have been. So in ending, I should like to make an exception of the film industry censoring system, which is designed less to stop us seeing what we want to see than to keep its own house in order. By and large, society has been happy to trust in the guidelines laid down by the industry, and apart from some rather ludicrous directives from the Hays Office in America before the last war, these 'watchdogs' have generally behaved with intelligence and sensitivity.

In 1970, John Trevelyan, then secretary of the British Board of Film Censors and one of the most enlightened in its history, used his influence to side with producers in dealing with an idiosyncracy in the law, an occasion commemorated as 'Trevelyan's Finest Hour' in an article by the journalist David Robinson in *Sight and Sound*. The fuss was over Andy Warhol's offbeat and much praised film *Flesh*, which had not yet been issued with a Board certificate for public showing, but which the Board considered entirely suitable for restricted audiences, ie, for screening at a licensed club, in this case the Open Space Theatre Club, sponsored by the government's Arts Council.

In February of that year, a massive police raid on the club (on the sort of scale associated today with quelling civil unrest), confiscated film and projector, suggesting an impending prosecution for obscenity. Trevelyan and others defended the film, pointing out that the law did not allow for an obscenity charge, even if the film was pornographic, which it was *not*. After questions in Parliament, the local police got cold feet, but tried to save face when they discovered that a few people in the audience were not members of the theatre club. The Greater London Council, which had licensed the club, was prevailed upon to bring summonses for 'failing to observe club regulations', and the case was heard at Hampstead magistrates court, where the bench considered the whole matter quite sordid and distasteful. Predictably they fined the club's two directors £100 each, and made them pay the costs of the prosecution. This was not an inconsiderable sum to a club struggling to survive, and Trevelyan suggested that Andy Warhol be asked if he would pay, which that gentleman was delighted to do 'in the fight against censorship'. The Board subsequently awarded the film an X certificate for public showing.

But irrespective of what censors (wise or unwise) may think, as I said at the outset everything depends on what turns you on. It is not uncommon for men and women to be stimulated by the very opposite of what we have been talking about – purity and chastity. At one extreme, who is to say that a nun's totally obsessive love for Christ, or a zealot's desire to scourge himself in pentitence, does not have sexual connotations? In literature the purity of the Arthurian knights (those that did not go in for rape and sexual adventures!) was presented as a counterpoint to the hedonism of others and a challenge to the various seductresses portrayed by Malory and others. Although spirituality usually manages to overcome the attractions of sex, the images conjured up are undoubtedly erotic to a number of people. Does this mean that some future censor will look a little closer at the books that recount the lives of the gallant ladies and gentlemen of past epics? I hope not.

12
Looking For Erotic Books

As I suggested in the preface, erotic books published before the twentieth century are not easy to find. The destruction of collections by well-intentioned philistine relatives on the death of the bibliophile has accelerated the decimation caused by the ravages of time that one has come to expect. Then, after the demands of the libraries and private collections, there is little left to circulate. However, much of the excitement of collecting lies in the *search* for elusive material, and it is possible to start from scratch with the assistance of your antiquarian bookseller or, preferably, several bookdealers.

While most bibliophiles collect for the pleasure it brings, and not for financial reasons, collectors should not lose sight of re-sale values, and therefore it pays to adhere to certain principles, such as aiming at first editions. The truly dedicated make life more difficult by starting even earlier with pre-publication versions, such as printer's proofs and author's manuscripts – but this is scarcely practical in the case of the so-called classics. More realistically, first English-language translations (in the case of foreign books), or first 'modern' editions of very old books, can present a worthy challenge in themselves.

Since many collectors define their interest as 'anything' on the subject, it makes sense to start with whatever happens to be available in the first instance, especially if (as one hopes) you intend to read the material and then discard reprints as the originals come to light. In fact some collectors are not satisfied until they have a copy of every imprint, paperback as well as hardcover.

Many of the titles listed below are out of print but should not be too difficult to find on the secondhand/antiquarian market; others (Henry Miller, for instance) are kept in print because of the constant interest in his work. In the case of older 'classics', rare early editions are invariably costly collectors' items, but there is usually a selection of reprints, published over the years 'privately' and often in limited edition. Again, in collecting terms, a limited edition is by its very nature a desirable item and, given the choice, one looks for aesthetic satisfaction in such features as the quality of paper and binding, the typeface and the illustrations. The examples given below are mainly editions I happen to have in my small collection, and are not expensive.

The danger in comparing the merits of different limited editions is that one becomes preoccupied with the book as an *objet d'art* and loses sight of the content. For example, short of reading the complete text, it is not easy to match the quality of the author's original words when there has been a translation. Many of them have been expurgated to the extent that the classification 'erotica' can be applied only loosely. This is true, for example, of de Brantôme's *Gallant Ladies* and de la Bretonne's *Sara*.

Restif de la Bretonne is to incest what de Sade was to sadism, although he would have been horrified by the comparison since he disapproved strongly of his contemporary's writing as well as his behaviour. He seems, apart from his fascination for incest, to have been a moral man and certainly treated women with respect, writing about them in idealistic terms. His *Monsieur Nicolas*, first translated into English by Havelock Ellis, was considered scandalous even in France, but *Sara*, which is the twelfth volume of that book, comes across as a simple love story by today's standards. Incidentally, the publisher of my edition – John Rodker – was also a bookseller and probably the inspiration for Graham Greene's bookseller in *The Human Factor*.

The odds against unearthing the lesser-known, typical Victorian erotica are longer, but well within the bounds of possibility. I have mentioned only four, but reference to one of the bibliographical works listed earlier, such as Alfred Rose's *Register*, will identify hundreds of others, although if you are restricted to English the field is again narrowed. I have, of course, restricted my list to English-language editions, which has meant leaving out many interesting books which have not been satisfactorily translated. It is difficult, for example, to find a good translation of Marguerite of Navarre's *Heptameron*.

Finally, an interest in erotica is very personal, and since the principal requirement for every acquisition is *quality*, you will inevitably have your own ideas. Some of the best erotica has been created by good writers almost unconsciously when the passage in question is an integral part of the greater creative process, and when integrity has added lustre to their talent.

Some Scarcer Titles and Editions

Anon, *Les Cents Nouvelles Nouvelles*, London 1899

Anon (pseudonym Lord Byron), *Don Leon*, London 1866 and Fortune Press, London 1934

Anon (pseudonym Lord Byron), *Leon to Annabella*, London 1866 and Fortune Press, London 1934

Anon, *The Lustful Turk*, London 1828

Anon, *Memoirs of Dolly Morton*, Philadelphia 1904

Anon, *The Modern Rake, or the Life and Adventures of Sir Edward Walford*, London 1824

Anon (Lord George Herbert), *A Night in a Moorish Harem*, Erotica Biblion Society of London and New York, nd (c1904)

Apuleius, *The Golden Ass* (*trans* William Adlington), Abbey Library, London, nd

Aretino, Pietro, *Works*. The shortage of good translations restricts my suggestions to the choice of:

The Ragionamenti or Dialogues of, 6 vols, Paris 1889

Dialogues (the Works of), privately printed by Rarity Press, New York 1931

Aristophanes, *Lysistrata* (verse by Jack Lindsay, illus Norman Lindsay), Sydney 1925, London 1926

The Arabian Nights' Entertainment, The Book of a Thousand Nights and a Night (*trans* Sir Richard Burton), 17 vols privately printed by the Burton Club, London 1885–8

The Book of a Thousand Nights and One Night (*trans* J. C. Mardrus and Powys Mathers), privately printed by the Casanova Society, 8 vols, London 1923; 4 vols, Routledge 1947

Balzac, Honoré de, *Droll Stories* (*illus* Robida), privately printed London, nd (c 1875)

Barrin, J., *Venus in the Cloister* (first trans from the French), London 1683

Boccaccio, Giovanni, *The Decameron* (illus Louis Challon), 2 vols, privately printed for the Navarre Society, 1921
de Brantôme, Pierre de Bourdeille, *Lives of Fair and Gallant Ladies*, first English-language edition, 2 vols, Paris 1901–2
de Brantôme, Pierre de Bourdeille, *Lives of Fair and Gallant Ladies*, 2 vols, Alexandrian Society, London and New York 1922 (limited to 1,250 copies
de la Bretonne, Restif, *Sara*, John Rodker for subscribers, London 1927 (limited to 1,000 copies)
Cabell, James Branch, *Jurgen*, Bodley Head, London 1921; limited edition, illustrated/unillustrated, 1923
Casanova, G. de Seingalt, *Memoirs* (*trans* Arthur Machen), 12 vols, privately printed London, 1922
Casanova, G. de Seingalt, *Memoirs* (drawings by Vincente Minnelli), 1 vol, Willey, New York 1946
Cleland, John, *Fanny Hill: the Memoirs of a Woman of Pleasure*, London 1748–9 (frequently reprinted)
Dryden, J., *Sylvia the Fair*, in *The Works of*, London 1808; *The Poems of*, *ed* Kinsley, J., Oxford 1955
Emmons, Earl H., *The Twin Buttes*, Peter Pauper Press, New York, nd
Herrick, R., 'The Vine', 'Show Me Thy Feet', in *The Poems of*, *ed* Martin, L. C., London 1965
Marlowe, C., and Chapman, *Hero and Leander*, included in *Works of Marlowe*, London 1885, and reprints
Olympia, *The Best of Olympia* (Olympia Press), New English Library 1966
Rabe, Claire, 'Sicily Enough', included in *The Best of Olympia*, New English Library 1966
Sacher-Masoch, Leopold von, *Venus in Furs*, Uranian Society, Boston 1925
Rochester, John Wilmot, 2nd Earl of, 'The Imperfect Enjoyment', et al, several 18th and 19th century editions; see Greene, G., *Lord Rochester's Monkey*, London 1974
Sellon, Edward, *The Ups and Downs of Life*, London 1867
Sherwood, James, *Stradella* (Olympia Press), New English Library 1966
Thompson, George, *The Delights of Love*, Farrell, New York, nd

Twain, Mark, *1601* (included in *The Best of Olympia*), New English Library, 1966
Wang Shih-Cheng, *The Golden Lotus* (*trans* Clement Egerton), 4 vols, Routledge, London 1957
Whitman, Walt, *Leaves of Grass*, New York 1855 and reprints
Wilkes, John, *An Essay on Women*, Aberdeen 1788
Wilson, Mary, *The Voluptarian Cabinet*, London 1824

Some Frequently Reprinted (and Paperback) Titles

Anon, *My Secret Life*, Panther Books, London 1972
Arsan, Emmanuelle, *Laure*, Mayflower paperback, 1976
Chaucher, Geoffrey, *The Canterbury Tales*, many editions including Penguin paperback
Hall, Radclyffe, *The Well of Loneliness*, Cape 1928
Harris, Frank, *My Life and Loves*, vol 1 etc, privately printed Paris, 1921
Humes, H. L., *Men Die*, Heinemann 1960
James, Norah, *Sleeveless Errand*, Scholartis Press 1929
Joyce, James, *Ulysses*, Bodley Head, London 1952
Kauffmann, Stanley, *The Philanderer*, Secker and Warburg, London 1953
Lawrence, D. H., *Lady Chatterley's Lover*, London 1928, Penguin 1960, reprinted with intro by Richard Hoggart 1961
Lyons, Nan and Ivan, *Someone is Killing the Great Chefs of Europe*, Cape 1976
Miller, Henry, *Tropic of Cancer*; *Tropic of Capricorn*, Paris; reprinted Calder 1960s
Nin, Anaïs, *The Journals of*, Owen, vols 1–6, London 1960s–70s
Nin, Anaïs, *Cities of the Interior*, Owen, London 1979
Nin, Anaïs, *Delta of Venus*, W. H. Allen, London 1978
Nye, Robert, *Falstaff*, Hamish Hamilton, London 1976, Sphere paperback 1978
Pepys, Samuel, *Diaries*, vols 1–9, Bell, London 1970–76
Réage, Pauline, *The Story of O*, Olympia Press, London 1970, Corgi paperback 1972
Rhinehart, Luke, *The Dice Man*, Talmy, Franklin, London 1971, Panther paperback 1972
Shakespeare, William, *Venus and Adonis* (any *Works* of Shakespeare)

Sharpe, Tom, *Porterhouse Blue*; *Riotous Assembly*; *Indecent Exposure*; *Blott on the Landscape; Wilt*, all Secker and Warburg/Pan paperback

Southern, T. and Hoffenberg, M., *Candy*, Geis, London 1968

Thomas, Leslie, *The Man with the Power*, Eyre Methuen, London 1973, Pan paperback

Wilson, Edmund, *Memoirs of Hecate County*, Doubleday, New York, 1946

Zola, Emile, *Nana*, reprinted many times; a good illus edition is in the Living Library series, World Publishing Co, USA 1946. Most of Zola's works are readily available, but the more dramatic the story and Zola's treatment, eg in *Earth*, the more carefully the translation should be examined. Some have no more bite than a TV 'Crossroads' instalment.

Source Material

Ashbee, H. W. (pseudonym: Pisanus Fraxi), *Index Librorum Prohibitorum*, privately printed London, 1877

——, *Centuria Librorum Absconditorum*, London, 1879

——, *Catena Librorum Tacendorum*, London, 1885

Barke, James, *Pornography and Bawdry in Literature and Society*, London, 1959

Bowdler, Thomas (ed), *The Family Shakespeare*, 10 vols, London, 1825

Brittain, Vera, *Radclyffe Hall: a case of obscenity?*, Femina Books, London, 1968

Calder-Marshall, A., *Lewd, Blasphemous and Obscene*, Hutchinson, London, 1972

Craig, Alec, *The Banned Books of England* (foreword by E. M. Forster), Allen & Unwin, London, 1937

Curwen, Henry, *History of Booksellers*, Chatto & Windus, London, 1873

Duffy, Maureen, *The Erotic World of Faery*, Hodder & Stoughton, London, 1972

Edwardes, Allen, *The Jewel in the Lotus*, Julian Press, New York, 1959

Edwardes, A. and Masters, R., *The Cradle of Erotica*, Odyssey Press, 1970

Flügel, J. C., *Man, Morals and Society: A Psycho-analytical Study*, Duckworth, London, 1945

Foster, J. H., *Sex Variant Women in Literature*, Vantage Press, New York, 1956

Fryer, Peter, *Mrs Grundy. Studies in English Prudery*, Dobson, London, 1963

——, *Forbidden Books of the Victorians*, Odyssey Press, London, 1970
Greene, Graham, *Lord Rochester's Monkey*, Bodley Head, London, 1974
Montgomery Hyde, H., *A History of Pornography*, Heinemann, London, 1964
Kronhausen, E. and P., *Pornography & the Law*, New English Library, London, 1967
Kuh, Richard H., *Foolish Figleaves: Pornography in – and out of – court*, Macmillan, New York, 1967
Legman, Gershon, *The Horn Book*, Cape, 1970
——, (ed), *The Limerick*, Bell, New York, 1969
Loth, David, *The Erotic in Literature*, Secker & Warburg, London, 1961
McDonald, Edward, D., *A Bibliography of the Writings of D. H. Lawrence*, Philadelphia, 1925
Marcus, Steven, *The Other Victorians. A Study of Sexuality and Pornography in Mid-Nineteenth Century England*, Weidenfeld & Nicolson, London, 1966
Orioli, Pino, *Adventures of a Bookseller*, Chatto & Windus, London, 1938
Perrin, Noel, *Dr Bowdler's Legacy. A History of Expurgated Books in England & America*, Macmillan, London, 1969
Rember, Charles, *The End of Obscenity: The Trials of Lady Chatterley, Tropic of Cancer, Fanny Hill* (foreword by Norman Mailer), André Deutsch, London, 1969
Rolph, G. H., *The Trial of Lady Chatterley*, Penguin Books, Harmondsworth, 1961
Reade, Rolfe, S. (pseudonym for Alfred Rose), *Registrum Librorum Eroticorum*, 1936
Rose, Reade, *Register of Erotic Books*, 2 vols, New York, 1965
Rowse, A. L., *The Case Books of Simon Forman: Sex and Society in Shakespeare's Age*, Weidenfeld & Nicolson, London, 1974
Rugoff, Milton, *Prudery and Passion: Sexuality in Victorian America*, Hart-Davis, London, 1972
St John Stevas, N., *Obscenity and the Law*, Secker & Warburg, London, 1956
Scott, G. Ryley, *Into Whose Hands: An Examination of obscene libel,*

its legal, sociological and literary aspects, Swan, London, 1945
Simons, G. L., *Pornography Without Prejudice*, Abelard-Schuman, London, 1972
Thomas, Donald, *A Long Time Burning: A History of literary censorship in England*, Praeger, New York, 1969
Tynan, Kenneth, *A View of the English Stage*, Paladin, London, 1976
Unwin, Stanley, *The Truth About Publishing*, Allen & Unwin, London, 1929
Young, Wayland, *Eros Denied*, Weidenfeld & Nicolson, London, 1965
Wertham, Frank, *Seduction of the Innocents*, Rhinehart, New York, 1954

Acknowledgments

The author wishes to thank Charles Lister of Bosworth Books, David Cheshire (librarian) and Peter Webb (lecturer) of the Middlesex Polytechnic Arts Faculty at Southgate, for their advice and assistance in the selection of illustrations; also Bosworth Books, The British Library, and Raymond O'Shea for permission to use certain illustrations.

For permission to quote from the works of various writers I have to thank the following: Laurence Pollinger Ltd and the Estate of the late Mrs Frieda Lawrence Ravagli (D. H. Lawrence, *Lady Chatterley's Lover*); A. M. Heath & Co Ltd and the Estate of the late Radclyffe Hall (Radclyffe Hall, *The Well of Loneliness*); John Calder Ltd (Henry Miller, *Tropic of Capricorn*); Stanley Kauffmann (Stanley Kauffmann, *The Philanderer*, copyright 1952, 1980); Routledge & Kegan Paul Ltd (Egerton, *The Golden Lotus*); The Society of Authors and the Estate of James Joyce (James Joyce, *Finnegans Wake*); W. H. Allen & Co Ltd (Anaïs Nin, *Delta of Venus*); Hamish Hamilton Ltd (Robert Nye, *Falstaff*); Eyre Methuen Ltd (Leslie Thomas, *The Man With the Power*); Talmy, Franklin Ltd (Luke Rhinehart; *The Dice Man*); Jonathan Cape Ltd (Nan and Ivan Lyons, *Someone is killing the great chefs of Europe*); Societe Nouvelle des Editions Jean-Jacques Pauvert (Pauline Reage, *The Story of O*).

Index

Adventures of a Bookseller, 24
Adventures of Huckleberry Finn, The, 18
Alcestis, 6
d'Angoulême, Marguerite, *see* Margaret of Navarre
Apuleius, Lucius, 65, 66-8
Arabian Nights, The, 73, 183
Aretino, Pietro, 78-80, 171
Aristophanes, 62
Ars Amatoria, 63
Ashbee, Henry, Spencer, 161, 167, 179, 182
Augustus, 63

Barke, James, 21
Baudelaire, Charles, 115
Beardsley, Aubrey, 25, 175-6
Beckett, Samuel, 8
Bessie Collier, 121
Best of Olympia, The, 178
Bible, the, 62
Bibliothèque Nationale, 182
Bierce, Ambrose, 15
Bijoux Indiscrets, Les, 144
Biron, Sir Charles, 38
Blott on the Landscape, 145
Boccaccio, Giovanni, 69
Biosgobey, Fortuné du, 110
Boucher, François, 174
Bowdler, Thomas, 16
Dr Bowdler's Legacy, 17
Bowra, C.M., 167
Boy, 120
Brantôme, Seigneur de, 80-1, 187
Bretonne, Restif de la, 187
British Board of Film Censors, 184
British Library, 182
British Museum, 179
Buckingham, 2nd Duke, 92-5
Burgess, Anthony, 117
Burns, Robert, 98, 105
Burton, Sir Richard, 183
Byron, Lord, 105

Cabell, James Branch, 30, 117-20
Campbell, Lord Chief Justice, 37
Candy, 146-8
Canterbury Tales, The, 71-2
Caracci, Agostino, 24; the family, 171-2
Carpenter, Edward, 121
Carpetbaggers, The, 10
Carrington, Charles, 163, 176-7
Casanova, 101-2
Case Books of Simon Forman: Sex and Society in Shakespeare's Age, 12-13
Catena Librorum Tacendorum, 161
Cather, Willa, 18
Catholic Office of Decent Literature, 30
Cent Nouvelles Nouvelles, Les, 73-8
Centuria Librorum Absconditorum, 161
Chandler, Raymond, 136
Chapman, George, 82
Charles II, 14, 88
Chase, James Hadley, 169
Chaucer, 71
Cleland, John, 99
Clemens, Samuel, *see* Twain, Mark
Cockroft, George, *see* Rhinehart, Luke
Comstock, Anthony, 24
Coward, Sir Noel, 130
Cruikshank, George, 174
cunt, 42 (excluding quoted matter)
Curll, Edmund, 25-7, 174
Curwen, Henry, 26

Decameron, The, 69-71
Defoe, Daniel, 18
Delights of Love, The, 165-6
Delta of Venus, 123-6
Dice Man, The, 7, 116, 132-4, 152-3
Diderot, Denis, 144
Dolly Morton, Memoirs of, 163-4

Don Leon, 105-6
Douglas, James, 36-7
Dryden, J., 92, 95-6
Du Barry, Mme, 174
Dugdale, William, 176
Dunbar, William, 21

Elephantis, 65
Eliot, T.S., 49
Elizabeth I, 31, 83
Ellis, Havelock, 36, 187
Emmons, Earl H., 155-6
Eros Denied, 56
Euripides, 6
Exeter Book, the, 68-9

Falstaff, 153-4
Family Shakespeare, 16
Fanny Greeley, 166
Fanny Hill, 99-100
Ferdinando, Paul, 176
Fielding, Henry, 17, 29
Fifteen Plagues of a Maidenhead, The, 25
Finnegan's Wake, 117
flagellation, 158
Flesh, 18
Forman, Simon, 12-13
Fragonard, Jean, 174
France, Anatole, 23
Franklin, Benjamin, 97-8
Fraxi, Pisanus, *see* Ashbee
Freud, Sigmund, 7
fuck, 21, 22, 42 (excluding quoted matter)

Gabler, Dr. Hans, 117
Gaboriau, Emil, 110
Gillray, James, 172
Girodias, Maurice, 8, 126, 177-9
Glinto, Darcy, 169
Golden Ass, The, 65, 66-8
Golden Lotus, The, 83-4, 152
Grassal, George, 163
Graves, Robert, 61, 65
Greek Passion, The, 183
Greene, Graham, 89, 142
Grove Press, 49
Grundy, Mrs, 14, 16
Gulliver's Travels, 17

Hall, Radclyffe, 25, 31-42, 44
Hankey, Frederick, 179-80
Hanley, James, 120
'Harlot's Progress, The', 172
Harris, Frank, 162-3, 174
Hays Office, 184
Heptameron, The, 72, 187
Here Lies John Penis, 120
Hero and Leander, 82-3
Herrick, Robert, 87-8
Hirschfield, Dr Magnus, 182
History of Booksellers, 26
History of the Decline and Fall of the Roman Empire, 16
Hoffenberg, Mason, 146-8
Hogarth, William, 172
Horn Book, The, 6, 98, 106, 161
Hotten, Joseph Camden, 173, 176-7
Humes, H.L., 130-1
Huntington, Henry E., 182

'Imperfect Enjoyment, The', 90-2
Indecent Exposure, 143-4
Index Librorum Prohiborum, 161

James, Henry, 109
Jameson, Storm, 130
Jane Eyre, 183
Jones, Henry Arthur, 28
Journals, 122
Joyce, James, 8, 48, 116-17
Joynson-Hicks, Sir William, 38
Jurgen, 117-20
Juvenal, 65

Kama Sutra, 158, 183
Kauffmann, Stanley, 25, 55-60
Kazantzakis, Nikos, 183
Kinsey, Dr Alfred, 182
Kronhausen, Eberhart and Phyllis, 162

Lady Chatterley's Lover, 25, 42, 43-8, 49
Lady Don't Turn Over, 169
Lady Of The Camellias, 37
La Terre, 109
Lawrence, D.H., 25, 31, 42, 43-8, 55, 123, 157, 183
Leaves of Grass, 108-9
Legman, Gershon, 6, 98, 106, 154, 161
Leofric, Bishop of Exeter, 68
Leon to Annabella, 105
Library Association, The, 183
Library of Congress (Washington), 182
limerick, 10, 154-5
Limerick, The, 154
Little Review, The, 116
Lives of the Fair and Gallant Ladies, 80-1, 187

Lord Chamberlain, 28-9
Love's Coming of Age, 121
Lustful Turk, The, 158-9
Lyons, Nan and Ivan, 149-51
Lysistrata, 25, 62-3, 175

Malory, 185
Man and Superman, 24
Man with the Power, The, 134-8
Marcus, Steven, 160
Margaret of Navarre, 72, 80, 123, 187
Marlow, Christopher, 82-3
'Marriage a la Mode', 172
Masoch, Leopold von Sacher, 111-15
Maupassant, Guy de, 109
Men Die, 130-1
Merry Muses of Caledonia, 98
Methodist Times, 109
Miller, Henry, 25, 48-55, 122-3, 126-7, 186
Miller's Tale, The, 71-2
Miss Callaghan Comes to Grief, 169
Moby Dick, 18
Moll Flanders, 18
Monkton-Milnes, Richard, 181
Monsieur Nicolas, 187
Montalk, Geoffrey de, 120
Morton, Thomas, 14
Motte, Benjamin, 17
Mrs Warren's Profession, 23
My Life and Loves, 162-3
My Secret Life, 160-2

Nabokov, Vladimir, 8
New York Times, 24
New York Times Book Review, 122
Nights in a Moorish Harem, A, 160
Nights of Horror, 170
Nin, Anaïs, 49, 122-6, 157
Nye, Robert, 153-4

Obscene Publications Acts, 39, 42
Observer, The, 117
Olympia Press, 8, 126, 178
Orioli, Pino, 24
Orwell, George, 49
Osborne, John, 29
Other Victorians, The, 160
Ovid, 63-4, 82

Pepys, Samuel, 11-12, 87
'Perfect Enjoyment, The', 93-4
Perfumed Garden, The, 158
Perrin, Noel, 17-18
Petronius, Cains, 65
Pierpoint Morgan, J., 182
Philanderer, The, 25, 55-60
Plumptre, Rev. James, 17
Poems and Ballads, 115
Pope, Alexander, 16, 27
Pornography and Bawdry in Literature and Society, 21
Pornography and the Law, 162
Porterhouse Blue, 144-5
Pretty Little Games, 173
Pygmalion, 23

Rabe, Claire, 126-7
Rabelais, François, 72, 123
Raimondi, Marcantonio, 78
The Rainbow, 43
'Rakes Progress, The', 172
Rêage, Pauline, 138-42
Rebell, Hughes *see* Grassal
Registrum Librorum Eroticorum, 6, 187
Renaissance, the, 69
Rhinehart, Luke, 7, 116, 132-4, 152-3
Riotous Assembly, 143-4
Robbins, Harold, 10-11, 63
Robinson Crusoe, 18
Rochester, 2nd Earl, 13-14, 89-92, 175
Romano, Giulio, 24, 78, 171
Rops, Felicien, 175
Rose, Alfred, 187
Rowlandson, Thomas, 172-4
Rowse, A.L., 12
Ruskin, John, 174

Sade, Marquis de, 105, 170
Sadleir, Michael, 182
Salome, 175
Sapper, 170
Sara, 187
Satires (of Juvenal), 65
Satyricon, The, 65
Savoy, The, 176
School of Venus, The, 100
Sellon, Edward, 167-9
Shakespeare, William, 71, 81-2
Sharpe, Tom, 143-5
Shaw, George Bernard, 23-4, 39, 56, 163
Sherwood, James, 127-9
Sicily Enough, 126-7
Signor Dildoe, 89-90
1601, 18-20
Smith, Wallace, 121
Smithers, Leonard, 177
Society, 111

Societies for the Reformation of Manners, The, 11
Society for the Suppression of Vice, 24, 30
Sodom, 13-14
Someone is Killing the Great Chefs of Europe, 149-51
Song of Solomon, 62
Sophocles, 62
Southern, Terry, 146-8
Stable, Mr Justice, 56
Stephenson, Sir A.K., 110
Story of O, The, 105, 115, 138-42
Story of Venus and Tannhauser, The, 176
Stradella, 127-9
Stubbs, John, 31
Suetonius, 65
Sunday Express, 36-7
Swinburne, Charles, 115
Swift, Jonathan, 17, 65

Thomas, Leslie, 134-8
Thompson, George, 165-6
Thousand and one Nights, The, see Arabian Nights
Tiberius, 64-5
Times, The, 110
'To Celia', 92-3
To Deprave and Corrupt, 8
Tom Brown's Schooldays, 18
Tom Jones, 17
Toulouse-Lautrec, 175
Trevelyan, John, 184
Tropic of Cancer, 49
Tropic of Capricorn, 25, 48-55
Turner, J.M.W., 174
Twain, Mark, 18-19
Twin Buttes, The, 155
Tynan, Kenneth, 28

Ulysses, 48, 116-17
Underground City, The, 130
Unwin, Stanley, 121
Ups and Downs of Life, The, 167-9
Utamaro, 175

Vatican Library, 182
Venus and Adonis, 91-2
Venus in Furs, 111-15
Venus in the Cloister, 25
Verlaine, Paul, 157
Villiers, George, *see* Buckingham
'The Vine', 88
Vizetelly, Henry, 109-10
Voltaire, 7, 97
Voluptarian Cabinet, The, 107

Walpole, Hugh, 120
'Walter', 160, 162
Ward, Rev. V., 38
Warhol, Andy, 184
Waugh, Evelyn, 143
Well of Loneliness, The, 25, 31-42
Wertham, Dr Frank, 170
Whitman, Walt, 108-9, 111
Wife of Bath, The, 72
Wilde, Oscar, 37, 175
Wilkes, John, 100-1, 120
Wilmot, John, *see* Rochester
Wilt, 145
Wish, The, 13
Wodehouse, P.G., 143

Yates, Dornford, 170
Young, Wayland, 56

Zola, Emil, 63, 109-11